DOROTHY SHUTTLEWORTH

HER LIFE & TIMES AT OLD WARDEN

WRITTEN BY
HER GRANDDAUGHTER CHARLOTTE

First Published 2017

The Shuttleworth Trust
Old Warden Park, Bedfordshire, SG18 9EP

www.shuttleworth.org

ISBN 978 0 901319 31 9

Typesetting & Origination by David Sheppard
Proworx Media Limited, Castleworks, Westgate Street, Lewes, East Sussex BN71YR

Printed in the UK.

For Dorothy by her elder granddaughter, Charlotte

Thanks and Acknowledgements:

I am most indebted to those who have helped me by the research they have done on my behalf, be it on the internet or by visits to the Bedford County Archives where many papers from Old Warden Park are stored and catalogued.

Here my heartfelt thanks go to Christine Hill whose knowledge of Old Warden is ingrained in her being and her professional use of the Internet has proved invaluable. Her book 'Tenants and Squires' which I can recommend to be read in conjunction with this life of Dorothy gives far more information on the village than I have done.

My thanks also to Val Bramley who is courageously filing the archives kept at Old Warden House itself and who seems to have a direct link to all national newspapers, in particular those in Bedfordshire where press reports going back well over 120 years have been most illuminating. Major Benjamin at the Archives of the Collection has also been most helpful in supplying details where cars and aeroplanes are mentioned as well as supplying me with information regarding the Cambridgeshire and the Oakley Hunts.

My own memories have been collaborated by talking to family members and remembering activities in my childhood with friends of the family, as well as newly discovered cousins who somehow were unknown to me during my childhood years, particularly to Julian Lang whose collection of old photograph albums and family trees has been most enlightening, as well as Christian Lang, an expert genealogist on the Lang family.

Talking to those living in the village of Old Warden has also brought many nearly forgotten memories to life as well as supplying me with facts and knowledge about those living in the village during my grandmother's life.

Finally my thanks to the The Richard Ormonde Shuttleworth Remembrance Trust (ROSRT) and to those working for the Trust who are enabling these partly chronological chapters to be brought out in book form, especially to Amanda Done who, as Manager of the House and Park, has co-ordinated the contacts between the Trust Offices and myself and, without whose assistance, I could hardly have launched this project and to whom I am greatly indebted, as well as to Ciara Harper, a very experienced publicity expert, who is coordinating the different aspects of text and photographs.

I hope that readers will gain an insight into the life and times of my grandmother, Dorothy Clotilda Shuttleworth, and gain some understanding of her wishes and intentions by creating the Trust in memory of her son, Richard.

Sources & Copyright

Ampthill Foto: Pages 149 (Left & Right), 178, 180. Commons.wikemedia.org: Pages 12, 167 Conde Nast: Page 172. Darren Harbar Photography: Pages 53, 54. Flight Magazine (1956): Page 179 Private: Pages 13, 14, 15, 20, 27, 28, 29, 31, 34 (L & R), 36, 45, 52 (L & R), 53, 58, 59, 61, 62 (T & B), 63, 64, 65, 68, 69 (L & R), 71, 73, 77, 80, 81, 82, 83, 84 (T & B), 88, 89, 91, 96, 97, 99, 103, 108 (T & B), 109, 111, 115, 119, 120, 126, 127 (B), 133, 141, 146, 148, 153, 174 (L & R), 175, 189. Sketch: Page 158. The Landmark Trust: Page 19. The Shuttleworth Trust Archives: Pages 10, 14, 22, 23 (T & B), 30, 35, 40 (T & B), 41 (T & B), 43, 44, 46 (T & B), 56 (T & B), 85, 86, 93 (T & B), 95, 117, 125 (T & B), 127 (T), 131, 135, 139, 144, 153, 155 (T & B), 163, 164, 166, 169, 171, 182, 184, 188. US Vogue: Page 176

Dorothy Clotilda Shuttleworth; her life and times at Old Warden

by her granddaughter Charlotte

Family Tree

John Allenby SHUTTLEWORTH 1756 -? = Rebecca NEWTON 1800 -?

Arthur LANG 1808-1883 = Sarah TICKELL 1812-1880

Benjamin TAYLER 1810-1875 = Elizabeth DONALLEN 1801-1853

Neil CAMPBELL of Ardnahow 1761-1814 = Marianne CAMPBELL of Glendaruel 1766- 1812?

William McCLAREN 1795-1863 = Mary BUTTERWORTH RUNCORN

Joseph SHUTTLEWORTH 1819-1883 = Sarah CLAYTON ? - 1849

Robert LANG (Rev) 1840-1908 = Adine Louise TAYLER 1839-1911

Archibald CAMPBELL VI of Glendaruel 1808-1875 = Christina McCLAREN 1829-1890

Frank SHUTTLEWORTH 1845-1913 = m. 1st DOROTHY m. 2nd CLOTILDA LANG 1879-1968 = Wiliam McCLAREN CAMPBELL 1864-1924

Richard Ormonde SHUTTLEWORTH 1909-1940

Anne Elspeth CAMPBELL 1917-1986 = Alexander Prince CROŸ 1912-2004

Charlotte 1938 — 3

Emma 1943 — 3

Maxim 1946 — 2

Dorothy has 14 great-great-grandchildren

Map of Bedforshire 1811

Chapter 1

Dorothy and her family

The story of the life and the times in which Dorothy Clotilda Lang lived have not been written about before. She founded the Richard Ormonde Shuttleworth Remembrance Trust in 1944 after the death of her son, Richard. As her elder grand-daughter, I had known her all my younger years, she having died when I was nearly 30. I have many memories of her and was certainly very influenced by her. I am very grateful for all she taught me and for what I was able to learn from her. The idea that her life should be documented has been with me for some years and, although I am not an author or a true historian, I believe that my memories, coupled with the research that has been done during this work, justify the chronicle of her life I have tried to put together. Researching her life and that of her family as well as those of the Shuttleworths and of my grandfather, William Campbell, has been of great interest for me. It has given me many insights to facts of which I was previously unaware, as well as great pleasure in discovery.

Unfortunately, very little written in Dorothy's own hand has survived, apart from the diary of the 1906 trip around the world but I am indebted to the generous help I have been accorded, and the information discovered from many different sources has given me personally much pleasure and even satisfaction. There is a large amount of photographs documenting many occasions and proving what a beauty Dorothy was aside from her strong, resilient and admirable character.

Dorothy Clotilda Lang was born on 7th July 1879 in Silsoe in the Flitton Hundredth of Bedfordshire as the younger daughter and sixth child of the Rev. Robert Lang and his wife, Adine. At the time of her birth, her father was the vicar

Silsoe Vicarage today where Dorothy Clotilda Shuttleworth was born 1879

of Silsoe and she was born in the pretty, late regency vicarage in the small, quiet, picturesque village adjoining the large estate of Wrest Park, the property of Lord de Grey. She had one sister and five brothers, only one of whom – Arthur - was younger than she.

In 1892, after a ten-year interim period in Harrow when her father was secretary for the Church Missionary Society, the Langs moved to Old Warden when her father was appointed vicar to the parish there. Old Warden is of no great distance from Silsoe and is also in Bedfordshire. She was just thirteen and she was to spend the rest of her long life at Old Warden.

The parish church had originally been built by the Cistercians of Warden Monastery only about a mile away across the fields and the Abbot had remained the patron until the Dissolution under Henry VIII. The monastery had been founded during the reign of King Stephen by Walter Espec, whose family already owned the land at the time of the Domesday Book and was a daughter house of Riveaulx. Shakespeare mentions 'hot Wardone Pies' made with the pears grown at the monastery and at present efforts are being made to revive the species. The church had been restored in the 1840s by Lord Ongley, the earlier owner of the Old Warden Estate. The picturesque village was also remodelled by him inspired by P.F. Robinson's book 'Village Architecture' of 1830. The cottages have small neogothic windows and thatched roofs, the front door being hidden at the back, tradition says to stop people gossiping.

Dorothy Clotilda Shuttleworth
with brother Harold, photo c.1883

The parsonage was a large and comfortable late Georgian house with extensive gardens, part of the picturesque village and only a short walking distance across the fields from St Leonard's Church. I can imagine that in those times a small country village must have appeared idyllic and tranquil after the years of travelling in which Dorothy's father had been involved. I do not remember her stating whether the enforced rural surroundings were a disappointment for Dorothy and her siblings after the years in Harrow which after all, is close to the busy capital city.

She seemed to become immediately steeped in the life here, involved with the village and the parish, helping her parents with any church fetes and meetings, learning to play both the piano and the organ which she continued to play all her life. Her father founded a monthly parish magazine and was still very close to the Church Missionary Society in which he had been active during those years in Harrow. He wrote and preached that to missionize was the first duty of a Christian and every household in the village was encouraged to have a money box to collect for the missions.

Dorothy continued to be educated at home by a governess, Miss C.M Feure, from Essex and was taught Greek and Latin as well as Algebra by her father whilst her elder brothers had been to different schools, Harrow and Charterhouse, and were all already students at Cambridge. She used to tell me about bicycling the 24 miles to visit them, admittedly over very flat countryside but, considering that

Lang brothers Charles Vaughan, Eustace, Frank, Harold & Arthur c.1890

The Vicarage, Old Warden, now known as Orchard Grange

Rev Robert Lang. Photoportrait c.1906

the bicycles of those years had no gears, it must have been quite a feat. As a younger daughter growing up with five brothers, she was probably quite sporty but I have not discovered whether she learnt to ride as a child although, as there were stables at the vicarage, riding or driving around in a dog-cart or some small carriage, must have been the usual form of transport. Certainly, she rode daily once she was married (only ever side-saddle) and did not give up riding until the Second World War. I still used to see her horse grazing in the meadows near the lodge gates when I was a small child.

She would tell me about her childhood, about the doll's she had, the necklaces she collected and also about escapades of her smaller brother, Arthur, the youngest of the family. Once he was given a box of chocolates by a guest and. when told to hand them around, he did so but said he had bitten into or licked every chocolate! Later he became a very gifted wood carver and often gave his nephews and nieces hand-made figures and I was once given a small wheel-barrow with a ball-bearing wheel which I still own.

When Frank Shuttleworth inherited the property after his father's death in 1883, he lived in the newly built Old Warden Park House and became very involved in village and County life. He was patron of the church and also a churchwarden, attending all parish meetings. He continued the work of embellishing the church and donated a new organ to celebrate the Diamond Jubilee of Queen Victoria in 1887 and he had the bells recast in 1899.

He would invite all his tenants to garden parties and fetes, with annual school treats for the children. Frank must have met the parson's family when they moved to Old Warden in 1892, if he had not already met them before. Frank and Robert Lang were of the same generation, both born in the 1840s. Dorothy, being the parson's daughter. obviously met and saw Frank after her family's arrival in the village and thereafter and there must have been regular contact between the Lang family and the Shuttleworths. Various events are described in the parish magazine where Dorothy either sings or plays the piano and even Frank performs on occasion too.

According to local word of mouth, the couple courted in the Swiss Garden, a very romantic location, and I can see that the pretty and well brought up daughter of the vicar was an appealing option for Frank. He was 57, had never been married, neither he nor his brother had children and he needed an heir. The women of his own generation were too old to have children and the daughters of his friends probably thought him too old so perhaps he fell in love with what Dorothy's younger brother Arthur cited "the sunbeam of Old Warden and the light of the village" - a romantic and Pygmalion-like project.

How Dorothy reacted probably no-one now knows. He must have been an attractive personality, despite being so much older, and closer to her father in age so did he whirl her off her feet, was she enticed by the glamorous life he led in society? Perhaps even the challenge of taking on the responsibility that she would have as the hostess of a large house and all that entailed, could, I wonder, have influenced her decision. She always said Frank was the love of her life and she revered him to the end of her days, always wearing a miniature of him in a blue lacquered gold locket hung around her neck on a gold and pearl chain until she died in 1968 at the age of 89.

Chapter 2

Frank Shuttleworth and his family

Frank was born in 1845, the younger of the two sons of Joseph Shuttleworth and his wife, Sarah Clayton, who was the sister of his business partner, Nathanicl Clayton. The Lincoln-based firm of Clayton and Shuttleworth built agricultural machinery and steam engines with factories in many different countries within Europe and the British Empire. They were very successful at the Great Exhibition in 1851 and won many prizes and awards and were employing about two thousand workers when Joseph died in 1883.

Alfred, Frank's elder brother, went to Rugby but Frank attended Dr Lovell's international school in Buckinghamshire. The school had been founded at Mannheim in Germany in 1836 as an English school, then moved to Britain and opened at Winslow in 1848. The liberal curriculum gave a classical, mathematical and scientific education with a rapid acquirement of the German and French languages, the students being drawn from various nationalities.

After graduating in the late 1850s, Frank continued his education with periods spent in both France and Germany improving his linguistic abilities. There is a scrap album full of photographs of his visits to different countries and he also seems to have often been in the Channel Islands as well as travelling throughout England and Scotland. The more I researched Frank's life, the more I was impressed by his very liberal and balanced views and can only appreciate how his family with their industrial background brought up their sons to be responsible and philanthropic members of society. This is also illustrated by the way Frank developed such a close friendship with all his tenants and employees, shown by their appreciation of him as a landlord and employer.

An engraving of the remains of Warden Abbey after it had been made a mansion house, and before it was demolished c.1790. *The current surviving fragment lies at the junction of the two wings, to either side of the barley twist chimney at the centre of the engraving. (S & N Buck,* A Description of England & Wales, *Vol. I, 1749).*

Warden Abbey Manor print 1730

After school, Frank went into the army and joined the 7th Hussars cavalry regiment and was gazetted in 1866, serving first in Ireland in Dublin and then he was posted to India with his regiment, sailing from Tilbury around the Cape of Good Hope to Bombay. On arrival, he volunteered for the Abyssinian war which had just erupted but was obliged to remain with his regiment in India. He made use of his time there by travelling widely.

In Kashmir, he shot Ibex and other game. When he returned to England in 1870, he changed to the 11th Hussars and, due to his proficiency in German, he was appointed interpreter to the German General Blumenthal who attended manoeuvers on Salisbury Plain. As a young officer of the 11th Hussars, Frank most likely attended the famously elaborate manoeuvres at Aldershot and Chobham in 1871 under the Duke of Cambridge, (of whom a portrait hangs at Old Warden) as well as under Gen. Sir James Hope-Grant who was married to a sister of Adine Lang, Dorothy's mother so I can imagine that possibly the Langs and Frank met through that contact, a slim link but it is possible that a social

Frank Shuttleworth photo by Speaight of Dicksee portrait

contact may have brought the Rev Lang to the notice of the patron of the living at Old Warden. As I have mentioned in Chapter 1, the Rev Robert and Frank Shuttleworth were of the same generation, both born in the 1840s with only five years difference.

In the archives at Old Warden there is a scrap album with every possible newspaper cutting about these manoeuvres where there was a widely reported stampede of horses and I presume Frank, serving in a cavalry regiment, may have been present. Frank served in the 11th Hussars for twelve years, advancing to becoming a major in 1882 before he retired on the death of his father in 1883 when he inherited the Old Warden estate. He moved to live there, taking his duties as the landowner seriously and becoming involved in the life of the village as well as of the estate as a whole. His step-mother, Caroline Jane, was still the hostess until her death in 1899.

Apart from Frank's business interests in the family firm of Clayton and Shuttleworth of which he was Chairman, he was also a Director of the Great Northern Railway Company. Frank was a Justice of the Peace and High Sheriff of Bedfordshire in 1891, he was also deputy Lieutenant of Bedfordshire and in 1901 helped raise the Bedfordshire Imperial Yeomanry of which he became honorary Colonel. Upon his appointment, he was presented to Edward VII who had just become King.

Frank was a great sportsman, riding in many steeplechases, winning eight out of fourteen he entered. He won the Grand Military at Punchestown wearing his personal racing colours of maroon with a black velvet cap and he twice won the Regimental Challenge Cup. He bred his own horses, the most famous of which was Matador, and was Joint Master of Foxhounds for the Cambridgeshire Hunt for 8 years. He was also involved in the Shire Horse Society and horses he bred held names beginning with 'Old Warden'.

Many of his horses are buried behind the Queen Anne's Summerhouse in the Warren at Old Warden, all with headstones giving their names and dates. There are also paintings in the house of some of the horses he bred and rode. He was renowned as a coach driver, winning several prizes as a member of the Four in Hand and Coaching Clubs. He was an excellent shot and developed the pheasant shoots at Old Warden holding three or four shoots a year, at which about 1,300 birds, both pheasants and partridges, were shot all documented with the list of guns and the bag in the Old Warden Guest Book. Frank was also a member of

Caroline Jane Shuttleworth, nee Ellison of Boulton Hall

many other clubs, in particular the Carlton, the Turf, the Bachelors', the Naval and Military and Cavalry Clubs. He featured in Vanity Fair 'Men of the Day' with a full-page cartoon and a long article.

Frank was an avid sailor and owned a series of yachts, maybe the most important of which was the Xarifa of 193ft length constructed by J. Samuel White of East Cowes. He used to spend the regatta week every August in Cowes, becoming a member of the Royal Yacht Squadron in 1888, when he owned the Primrose followed by the Oberon the next year and then the Mohawk in 1894, then the Paulina in 1895 followed by the Xarifa and then in 1900 he bought the Zaneta which was a screw steam yacht of 115 tons built in 1897. Finally, he had the Mera of 293 tons from 1904 until in 1912 he chartered the Portia for his last yachting season.

Cambridge Hunt meet at Old Warden Park

View of Old Warden Park, Frank Shuttleworth with dogs

In 1891, just a few years after becoming a member, Frank bought a large yellow brick house called Thornhill, just behind the RYS castle at a cost of £6,000. Part of its front garden was taken and added to the castle's lawn and the property was then sold, minus this strip of land, to another Squadron member, Lord Iveagh, for £4,000. The balance of £2,000 was paid to Frank by a special subscription among the Squadron members.

Frank Shuttleworth moved socially in the so-called Prince of Wales's set, meeting figures from society at many sporting events, be it racing or sailing. His circle of friends was very wide, many of whom attended the shoots at Old Warden or were invited on Frank's yacht during Cowes week. The guest book of his yachts, being signed by all who came aboard, shows how very cosmopolitan his friends were - the London society, the English aristocracy and international figures such as the exiled Empress Eugenie of France and the Infante Don Alfonso of Spain with his wife Beatrix, a granddaughter of Queen Victoria, as well as many French, Hungarian and German society figures of the time.

During the years when Dorothy was on board with him, they seem to have sailed to various destinations apart from the annual week in Cowes. They went to Salcombe, to Lulworth Cove, to the Scilly Isles, to Scotland, to Holland and even to the Mediterranean. The Marquess of Ormonde, who was the Commodore of the Royal Yacht Squadron was a regular guest and became Godfather to their son, Richard, when he was born in 1909 as was Lord Scarborough who was another old friend, having been the first to sign the guest book in 1888.

When Frank and Dorothy married in June 1902, coming home from their honeymoon as the new lady of the manor must have been a very poignant moment for Dorothy. Her parents were moving away, her father having swapped the parish with the previous vicar of Dinton near St Albans. I feel he did not want to remain at Old Warden as the father-in-law of the local squire and a man of his own age and perhaps wanted Dorothy to feel she was now a grown woman with new duties and only responsible to her new husband.

Robert Lang was a very tactful and discreet person also illustrated by the way he never played cricket again after being ordained despite his famous record as an extremely fast bowler both at school and at Cambridge. He must have given up cricket, which was nearly always played on Saturdays and Sundays, not wishing to be distracted from his duties holding the church services at weekends.

The two families came from very different backgrounds, the Langs with a long lineage reaching back to many historical figures in England's past with the traditions of serving the Almighty and the Country and the Shuttleworths who, just a few generations back, had been boat builders in Lincolnshire and had then with great acumen and business sense developed the thriving company of Clayton and Shuttleworth. Their enterprising understanding of mechanics enabled them to contribute to the growing industrialisation of the country. They had earned a fortune in two generations and were at the same time driven by a sense of responsibility, serving the local community and supporting philanthropic institutions so that when Joseph Shuttleworth decided to also acquire a landed estate, the members of the family automatically grew into being involved in the local institutions and took on the responsibilities of a good landlord.

Chapter 3

Dorothy's ancestors

Dorothy was very interested in history and she told me quite a lot about her ancestors. We are all the product of past generations whether we like to accept that or not and I see history as a woven tapestry where one can follow the threads through the centuries.

In earlier times, the Langs had come from Lancashire but, during the eighteenth century. Robert Lang (Dorothy's great grandfather) was a West Indian merchant and sailing to and from the New World must still have been a great adventure in those days. He owned many plantations on different Caribbean islands partly inherited from his wife's father and I fear that they had slaves working on them. I am not quite clear how the plantations came to be owned in that era and under whose jurisdiction they were. This Robert and his wife, Maria, had sixteen children and then moved to Moor Park near Farnham in Surrey. This was a large house which had been built in the late seventeenth century by the famous statesman, Sir William Temple who, at the time of William and Mary's accession to the throne, was instrumental in negotiating the so called 'bloodless revolution of 1688'. Memorial stones to various members of the Lang family can still be seen in the parish church. Robert was a great bibliophile and built up a famous library. He was a founder member of the Roxburghe Club from its beginning in 1812 until 1821.

The Roxburghe club was formed after the sale of the Duke of Roxburghe's library at an auction where a world record price was paid for a book, a 16th century manuscript by Boccaccio. Every member of the Club was supposed to have a facsimile of an important book of his printed to be offered to other members and to the wider public and Robert had fourteen books in all published. The Roxburghe club still exists to this day and is a most prestigious organisation, still true to its original intentions. Robert was also a friend of Sir Walter Scott, another founder member, who used to come and stay at Moor Park and sit in the ruins of Waverley Abbey nearby (inspiring him to write his Waverley novels). Regrettably Robert's son later organised an auction of the books in his library which lasted for four days and consisted of over one thousand lots.

Sarah Tickell wife of Arthur Lang

Maybe the fact that the Langs had had slaves on their plantations explains why a few generations later both Dorothy's father and her grandfather who worked for the East Indian Company became involved in the Church Missionary Society. This had been founded in 1799 by William Wilberforce and John Venn with a group of activist evangelical Christians to abolish the slave trade and to further social reform. The aims of the Society were then also to bring Christianity to the rest of the world. Arthur Lang, Dorothy's grandfather, considered an Anglo-Indian having lived in India for most of his professional life, became Vice President before his death in 1883. Thus, his son Robert was following in his father's footsteps by being appointed as one of the three secretaries to the CMS in 1881. Each secretary looked after different regions around the world. In the following years Robert travelled to Palestine, the Middle East and then to Africa but his health was affected after the strain of the Niger controversies so he resigned and then took on the parish of Old Warden.

Dorothy's family were of a very typical Victorian English background, both her parents and grandparents and even some of the great grandparents had been born in India, serving either first in the East India Company and later in the Indian Civil Service as high-ranking army officers, Commissioners, judges or even as medical doctors. They served in the north-western territories in India, on the borders of Afghanistan, moving with the government from Calcutta in the winters, to Simla in the summers. Others had tea plantations in Ceylon.

Most of these families sent their children back to England to be educated as in the case of Dorothy's father who was born in Jessore in 1840. This was the era when many boarding schools were founded and opened to cater for children returning alone from the distant reaches of the Empire. Travelling back and forth to India in the middle of the nineteenth century and before the Suez Canal was finally opened in 1869, was a long, slow and arduous procedure. Originally, it could take up to six months when sailing around the Cape then, when steam boats came into operation, the fastest route was to cross the English Channel, go by train through France to Marseille, there board a boat to sail across the Mediterranean to Alexandria and then take the so called overland route to board the next ship at a port on the Red Sea. Then, once in India, it could take another few weeks to arrive at the destination so that any trip in the middle of the 19th century must have taken nearly a year in all.

Eliza Donnallen, wife of
Benjamin Tayler, c.1920

When grown up, these children either joined the Indian Civil Service and returned to India or stayed in England where at that time there was not much choice regarding a career. If there was no family estate to inherit, the next option was to join the army or to enter the church and this was prevalent amongst Dorothy's ancestors. Her father was one of eleven siblings. His father, Arthur Moffatt Lang, served as a Judge with the East India Company and was married to Sarah, the daughter of Lt General Richard Tickell whose family had wide contacts in the eighteenth-century world of writers, poets and artists. Robert was first at a prep school in Weymouth in 1851 and then at Harrow where he started his successful cricket career. According to family tradition he was known as 'Bob the Bowler and is still sung about in the second verse of the Harrow school cricket song. He then went to Cambridge to Trinity College and here again cricket was an important part of his curriculum playing in the Cambridge University XI in 1852 where he famously took five wickets for four runs and four for thirty-one, the details of which can still be looked up in the Wisden Cricket Almanac. Robert studied theology at the Sacred College in Doncaster, was ordained a deacon in Carlisle in 1864 and then became a priest in Kendal.

Cambridge XI of 1862, in 1906

Standing left to right: C. Booth; Hon T de Grey (Lord Walsingham); Hon C G Lyttleton (Viscount Cobham); M.T.Martin (Rev.Cannon); W.Bury.
Sitting left to right: Rev.Robert Lang; Sir H.M.Plowden; H.M.Marshall. Deceased: AW.T.Daniel d.1873, G.F.Helm d.1898, H.W.Salter d.1884

From Robert's very neatly kept photograph albums, one can see that he travelled widely in Europe in the years 1865 and 1866, photographing all the famous cathedrals up the Rhine especially Cologne where the towers had just been finished, then into Switzerland and back through France. Also, in 1866, he was staying with Sir Robert and Lady Montgomery near Lynmouth to where they had retired, Sir Robert having been the Governor of the Punjab. There was some relationship between the Montgomerys and the Langs and Sir Robert also later became godfather to one of Robert's sons. (Field Marshall Montgomery who was a leading general in the Second World War was a grandson of that Sir Robert).

Adine Lang Tayler, Dorothy's mother 1848

Robert Lang seems to have been to India again to Allhalabad in 1866 and perhaps Adine Tayler's family were still there. Adine was born at Allhalabad in 1839, her father, Benjamin Tayler, serving in India as a judge in the North-West territories. Her mother, Elizabeth Donallen, was of Irish descent and had grown up in Capetown where there was a well-established Irish colony. She had married Benjamin Tayler there when he had stopped in Capetown on his way to India. The Taylers had five daughters, Adine being the second youngest. They were all born in India and were reputed to be great beauties. A watercolour of all the sisters still exists and there is a charming one of Adine surrounded by flowers painted in about 1860. There was also a younger brother who became a tea planter, it is thought in Ceylon, and he is buried beside his parents in the graveyard of St Leonard's Church at Old Warden.

Adine married the Rev Robert Lang in 1868 at Upton Park near Slough where her parents were then living having shortly retired from India. Robert's first parish was at Petworth from 1865-72, where their eldest son, Robert Charles Vaughan, was born.

Dorothy would recount how she was brought up on the story of how, during the Indian Mutiny in 1857, one of her mother's sisters, Aunt Kate, stood at the top of the steps leading to their house with a baby in one arm and a pistol in her other hand defending the family against the attacking mutineers. Another sister Jean's husband

– Mordaunt Ricketts, a magistrate – was the first white man to be killed at the beginning of the Mutiny during a church service. Yet another sister, Helen, was married to the famous General Sir James Hope-Grant who, together with General Sir Colin Campbell, recaptured Lucknow and put down the Mutiny. Arthur Moffat Lang, the elder brother of Robert, was a young lieutenant in the Bengal Engineers and played a leading role in breaching the defences at Lucknow and was nominated to receive the Victoria Cross for his bravery. (There is a memorial to him in the church at Old Warden.)

The Tayler sisters: Helen Lady Hope Grant, b.1826; Catherine Shakespeare b.1827; Jean Mordaunt b.1830; Mary Wise b.1834; Adine Louise Lang, b.1839

The Mutiny had broken out after use being made of the 'doctrine of lapse' whereby, should an heir to a territory not be a son of the ruling Indian family, the principality would be annexed by the leading power, in that case the East India Company. The sepoys who made up four fifths of the army also feared an imagined forced conversion to Christianity and, when new cartridges were issued where the cap had to be bitten off before being placed into the rifles, the rumour rapidly spread that they were sealed with animal fat which, if it was from cattle, was taboo to the Hindus for whom cows were sacred and, if with pork fat, was unclean to the Muslims.

The brutality of the rebellion was horrific with the slaughter of women and children at the massacre of Cawnpore and then the sieges of Lucknow and finally of Delhi which then led to the banishment of Bahadur Shah and the end of the Mogul Empire. A year later the East India Company came to an end and Great Britain took over its duties and obligations, founding the Indian Civil Service to replace the Company's agents and renounced the annexation policy although Britain continued to control the succession and assumed responsibility for 'protected' states.

Thus, Dorothy grew up with all these stories and heroic feats of her family so that they were very real to her and a part of her existence.

Chapter 4

Frank and Dorothy

Looking back now nearly one hundred and twenty years to when Frank and Dorothy married, I feel one must be reminded of what the world of which they were part was like at that time. Queen Victoria had died in January 1901, her long reign having given great stability to the country. She had been revered during her long reign as Queen and Empress as the country grew to be one of the most powerful nations of the world. When Dorothy was born in 1879, England was the acknowledged leading power. Queen Victoria was Empress of India from 1876, as well as being Queen of Great Britain and Ireland, and her Golden Jubilee was in 1887 when Dorothy was eight. Her eldest son, the Prince of Wales, was already nearly 60 when finally inheriting the monarchy as Edward VII. He was not crowned until two years later, after Frank and Dorothy were married, having had appendicitis when the coronation was to have taken place. He had been kept out of politics by his parents, particularly by the Queen and her ministers but he still achieved much influence, being related to most of the ruling families of the time and thus known as the Uncle of Europe and also, he was much respected due to his wide social contacts throughout the nation and he was welcomed as the new monarch, bringing in a somewhat lighter tone than his mother who had been a widow in mourning for the best part of the second half of the 19th century.

To further illustrate those times, I cite just a few historical and political developments which influenced life in that era, such as Edison's light bulbs transforming the lighting of towns, and his development of a telephone exchange after Bell patented his telephone in 1876, although telegrams had first been sent a few decades earlier. Greenwich Mean Time was adopted by Parliament, the Gotthard Tunnel joining Switzerland and Italy was completed and the Cathedral of Cologne in Germany was finally finished having been started in 1248. Stevenson had invented the first steam engine and, by the time Dorothy was born, railway lines had been laid throughout the country. On the political front, Gladstone was Prime Minister and had inaugurated universal education and founded the Trades Unions. His Tory counterpart, Disraeli, who had led a long political life, died in 1881. The Statue of Liberty was dedicated in New York in 1886. Unfortunately, wars and skirmishes were endemic in the widely spread Empire. The 2nd Boer War was coming to an end and the 2nd Anglo-Afghan War had ended in 1880. The Russian Tsar, Alexander II, in whom much hope had been held for a more liberal regime, had been assassinated in 1881 but tension in the relationship between the two countries continued even after the Crimean war, especially along the central Asian borders, despite the Tsar's daughter, Marie-Alexandrovna, being married to Queen Victoria's second son, the Duke of Edinburgh.

Frank and Dorothy's wedding

The marriage between Frank Shuttleworth and Dorothy Clotilda Lang took place at St Leonards Church at Old Warden, on 3rd June 1902, on a beautiful fresh early summer day. The happy atmosphere was also enhanced by the peace rejoicings at the prospect of ending the Boer War in South Africa which had lasted quite some years and both Dorothy and certainly Frank must have known friends serving in the army and involved in the war.

Dorothy was led to the altar and given away by her elder brother, Robert C. Vaughan Lang, as her father was officiating at the marriage ceremony. A detachment of the Bedfordshire Imperial Yeomanry had driven to the vicarage to accompany the bride to the church and ahead of her walked two sergeants with drawn swords. The guests were seated by two of her brothers, Frank and Arthur, together with a church warden, Mr Capon, and assisted by Frank's brother, Alfred Shuttleworth who was also the best man, and a friend, Mr Diggle. Four of Dorothy's friends were her bridesmaids (Evelyn Beatrice Edwards, Maud Ashfield, Muriel Osborn and Beatrix Greenfield) and the groom was attended by his elder brother, Alfred, and Sir Algernon Osborne – a neighbour. Dorothy's father, the vicar Robert Lang, assisted by his son Harold, a curate, and his own brother the Rev. James Thomason Lang, vicar of East Finchley, performed the marriage ceremony and the latter gave the address stressing the responsibility the couple were undertaking to serve the Almighty in word and deed and, as still

Dorothy Clotilda Shuttleworth, nee Lang
as a bride 1902

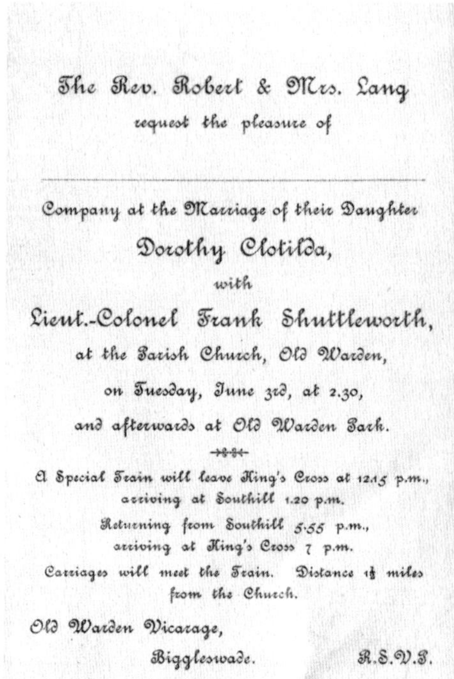

The Rev. Robert & Mrs. Lang
request the pleasure of

Company at the Marriage of their Daughter
Dorothy Clotilda,
with
Lieut.-Colonel Frank Shuttleworth,
at the Parish Church, Old Warden,
on Tuesday, June 3rd, at 2.30,
and afterwards at Old Warden Park.

A Special Train will leave King's Cross at 12.15 p.m.,
arriving at Southill 1.20 p.m.
Returning from Southill 5.55 p.m.,
arriving at King's Cross 7 p.m.
Carriages will meet the Train. Distance 1½ miles from the Church.

Old Warden Vicarage,
Biggleswade. R.S.V.P.

Dorothy & Frank wedding invitation 1902

traditional then, stressed that the wife be subject to her husband and obey him in all things.

Traditional wedding melodies were played by the organist from St Paul's church in Bedford who played Wagner's march from Lohengrin as the bride arrived. The flowers were done by Mr Modral, the head gardener from the House, famous for his arrangements. He decorated the church and made the arches on the route to the house. He also created the bride's bouquet of orchids, orange blossom, lilies of the valley and roses as well as doing the posies of Malmaison carnations carried by the bridesmaids. The bride's dress was of ivory satin trimmed with chiffon and real orange blossom with a silk tulle veil, and she wore the pearl necklace which was part of her wedding presents from Frank. The bridesmaids' dresses were of white muslin with black and white hats trimmed with clusters of roses and each had a diamond feather brooch given by the bridegroom.

The church with its dark carved pews was filled to the utmost, local families only being allowed to seat one member, all carefully watched over by the church

Dorothy & Frank wedding group 1902

wardens. The schoolchildren lined the churchyard, showering the bridal couple with flowers as they left the church and walked down the hill between an arch of lances held by the Yeomanry to their carriage which took them up to the House where there was a reception.

Dorothy & Frank wedding, 1902

A special train had brought guests from London and many neighbours and local dignitaries were also present. As was usual in those times, the papers reported in detail about the 200 wedding gifts which were displayed at the House. Frank gave Dorothy various items of jewellery such as the three-row set of pearls with an emerald clasp which she wore at the wedding, brooches and rings and a dressing-table set of tortoise-shell in a travelling case. She gave him a miniature in a locket and 'sleeve-links'. There were silver bowls and cups as well as a silver statuette of a Bedfordshire Yeoman from local organisations and a silver flower bowl and silver mirror frame (that stands on my dressing table today) from the tenantry, as well as many generous gifts from all the attending guests. The guest list was huge and, apart from all the attending relations and neighbours, included many friends from London and reads like Who's Who. The bridal couple received their guests in the House before passing through to a marquee which had been put up for the occasion and where tea was served. A huge wedding cake of about 5ft in height was on a stand in the centre, the cake magnificently decorated with the names of the couple in icing done by the well-known confectioners, Gunter's of London, whose tea rooms were just off Berkeley Square at that time and later in Curzon Street where they still were in my childhood and I even remember delicious sticky cakes eaten there.

Honeymoon

Frank and Dorothy left Old Warden for their honeymoon, driving in their carriage to the station in Biggleswade, escorted by the Yeomanry, then by train to

London where they stayed at the Grosvenor Hotel before leaving for Paris the next day. Frank gave Dorothy a small notebook to write a diary of the honeymoon. The first few days were spent in Paris where they stayed at the Ritz. They went sightseeing, shopping and attended the opera where they heard Faust and they drove to the Bois de Boulogne where there was a flower display after church on the Sunday. They dined with friends of Frank's most evenings and went to the leading restaurants and tea shops and also visited the embassy, as well as attending the race meeting at Auteuil and a polo game with Hungarian friends. A whirl!

Dorothy was somewhat overcome as she wept one evening, I presume slightly awed by the pace of life and the internationality of Frank's friends. I do not think she had ever been abroad before and she had hardly ever been to London, except to stay with relations for a short visit, having spent most of her childhood in Harrow or in small country villages. They left Paris twelve days later and were already dining with friends in London the same evening and with more friends and Frank's brother, Alfred, the following day. Dorothy went shopping with Lily Diggle, the wife of a close friend of Frank's, while Frank was at a board meeting and then they were on the way to Southampton to meet the yacht. It was windy and rainy but they immediately lunched with another friend on his yacht, the 'Crimson Rambler' and steamed around the Isle of Wight, dining on deck. At that time Frank owned the 'Zaneta', a screw steam yacht of 115 tons built in 1897, which he had bought in 1900. That week many friends must have visited them on board as the page in the yachts' guest book has many entries but, by the 24th June, they were in London again and staying with the Diggles when they heard that the Coronation was postponed because the new King Edward VII had appendicitis. The decorations were already up so Dorothy went around to look at them with her sister, Edith, then back they went to the yacht, sailed around the fleet and visited other yachts, the Miranda and the Paulina belonging to friends of Frank's. He had become a member of the Royal Yacht Squadron in 1888 and spent some time every year at Cowes on the different yachts he successively owned. Dorothy had her first birthday as a married woman on July 7th on the yacht which is noted in the guest book and Lord Ormonde, the Commodore of the Royal Yacht Squadron, dined on board with them. The following weeks they seem to have been up and down to London for Frank to attend meetings and to see friends and her parents dined on the yacht with them a few days after her birthday, as did the Duke of Somerset. A few days later they sailed to Swanage where they walked to the Globe and some caves and then bathed in the sea. Dorothy told me that she had to learn to swim that summer and was held in the water on a rope attached to a rod from the deck of the yacht. She seemed to be prepared to do anything new! They then sailed on to Falmouth, via Dartmouth, and to Salcombe where the Diggles left them to return home. At Falmouth, they shopped at Burton's Old Curiosity shop and bought some china vases and a toby jug. On 17th July, they sailed on to the Scilly Isles where they called on Mrs Dorrien-Smith who took them around her garden, famous for its tropical plants which grew there thanks to the proximity of the Gulf Stream. Dorothy had felt rather unwell as the yacht had pitched somewhat.

The rest of July continued in this vein, trips on the yacht, dinners, lunches, up to London for meetings and then they watched the postponed coronation on August 9th. A few days afterwards, they were back on the yacht and saw the fleet sail past in honour of the King and there was a review which other guests came on board to watch but, as it was so wet, they could hardly see anything. They then met the King, presumably at the Royal Yacht Squadron and Frank kissed his hand. Frank had had a nasty bought of influenza during those weeks and had to have a doctor visit him repeatedly. To us in these times the description of their honeymoon sounds more like a state visit than a romantic trip to enjoy being together but, to Dorothy, it was an introduction to the new life she was to lead.

Homecoming

Upon returning to Old Warden from their honeymoon which had lasted for two months, the home-coming was celebrated by the village as well as the tenants and local organisations. Whilst they were away, work had been done in the house with some rooms being re-decorated for the newlywed couple. As Frank and Dorothy drove in an open carriage from Biggleswade Station, crowds cheered their passing and the church bells pealed as they arrived at Old Warden village. Having reached the gates to the Park, the villagers unhitched the horses and drew the carriage themselves. A guard of honour formed by the Bedfordshire Imperial Yeomanry greeted them, and, later in the day, General Gatacre, Commander of the District, accompanied by his wife, came to inspect the Yeomanry. Again, a marquee was erected near the house and a meal was served for over 600 tenants and friends as well as over 200 yeomanry. Toasts and speeches were made, after which a sports event took place with all sorts of competitions, be it jumping, lemon cutting, tent pegging and flat and hurdle races of different lengths for both boys and girls, as well as for grown men.

Chapter 5

Old Warden Park and the Estate

Upon buying the Old Warden Estate in 1872, Joseph Shuttleworth commissioned Henry Clutton, a renowned architect, to make plans for a large country house to be reminiscent of the Jacobean Gawthorp Hall in Lancashire belonging to the Baron Kay-Shuttleworth of the time. After pulling down the old manor-house, Clutton, renowned for his 'Jacobethan' designs, built the imposing sandstone house in the centre of the historic parkland, situated in a dip of low-lying land close to the Greensand Ridge which crosses Bedfordshire from north east to south west. The building site being sand, Clutton, using Cubitts as builders, developed a very daring system of erecting a steel frame upon a concrete base of five feet in thickness, then facing the house in sand stone. Only a small wine cellar exists, which is possibly a remnant from the earlier house. The clock tower and the high chimneys of Tudor style added to the imposing aspect which was described in 1878 as a 'palatial residence on a moderate scale'. The high clock tower had four clock dials each of 6ft diameter. Five bells were cast by Taylor of Loughborough and the clock was built by Cook and Co. of York. Old Warden was Clutton's last country house, as his eyesight was failing but he still designed the new lodges at the entrances to the park, as well as the school in the village and restored some of the cottages placing the Shuttleworth crest with its motto Isto Velocior Vita – 'from swiftness comes life', on nearly all the buildings. He was assisted by a local architect and builder called John Usher with whom he had already worked restoring some of the churches on the Duke of Bedford's estate on the other side of the county.

By about 1880, the building of the new house was so far advanced that the Shuttleworths were able to move in. The interiors had been elegantly and grandly decorated with oak dado panelling in many of the rooms. There was a grand central oaken staircase with the walls painted Reckitts blue and embossed wallpapers and

View of Old Warden Park

House interior: Drawing Room

House interior: Saloon

House interior: Entrance Hall

plaster work panels and friezes in the other reception rooms. Most of the furniture was in oak matching the panelling in the reception rooms, the majority supplied by Gillows, a leading firm of that era. Upstairs, the bedrooms had suites of furniture in mahogany, some with painted flower designs. Most of the rooms had patterned Turkish rugs, the huge main hall carpet woven to fit the room with the Shuttleworth coat of arms in the centre. Joseph had bought many paintings by contemporary English artists - landscapes, oriental and historical scenes as well as paintings of hunting and animal scenes as influenced by Landseer, the leading artist of the period. Full length historic portraits were purchased for the saloon and the main stair hall. After Frank inherited and, when he married Dorothy, he had some of the rooms refurnished and newly decorated. He bought many eighteenth century English portraits at some of the leading art dealers in London such as Agnew's, Mallet's, and Partridge's, and at auctions at Christie's, as well as French Louis XV furniture which had once again become fashionable. The ground floor exclusively had reception rooms with the dining room, the drawing room and morning room all leading out of the central saloon lit from above by four glass domes. The saloon also had double doors opening into the grand entrance hall and further doors leading to other rooms and to the central staircase hall, from where separate steps lead to the billiard room, an addition built a few years later between the main house and the service east wing, where all kitchens, pantries, store rooms and servants quarters were placed. The layout of Old Warden was not easy, with just the small wine cellar under the East wing, and there was very little storage space in the house itself. There was not even a cloakroom on the main floor, just cupboards beside the front door. A series of utility rooms - the pantry, china room and silver vault with a walk-in safe open into a passage leading to the Garden Entrance.

The Service Wing which has a set of about twelve steps leading up to the ground floor, contained the butler's room, the still room, the flower room where also the dogs were washed and, at the end, was the large kitchen with game larder and a series of necessary storage rooms and cupboards for fresh vegetables and fruit. I think both the housekeeper and the butler had rooms leading off the main passage where all the bells for summoning servants are fixed to the wall, marked with the names of the rooms upstairs and downstairs. The first floor had a series of rooms used for the servants and the second floor which had a connection to the back stairs and so to the bedroom floor had the lady's maid's room, the linen room and a still room where my grandmother made her potpourri and her face creams and lotions.

Ongley House

Apart from the Swiss Garden laid out by Lord Ongley, the surroundings of the house were planned by the renowned garden architect, Edward Milner who, with his son-in-law Edward White had formed a company and laid out the public gardens in Lincoln and the gardens at Hartsholme Hall for Joseph Shuttleworth and so were employed again to design the park and the garden at Old Warden. The ha-ha surrounding the house and separating the gardens from the park was presumably his idea. It is to give the impression of the garden leading into the parkland without a separating wall or fence being visible and designed to prevent cattle and sheep wandering into the gardens. The land between the house and the lake was heightened to give a grander view across the park. To the west of the house, a formal garden was laid out surrounding a large red granite fountain. The ornate beds were later removed but one can still see the footprint of the flower beds from an upstairs window.

The romantic Swiss Garden where Dorothy and Frank courted was possibly planned and laid out in the early nineteenth century with (as mentioned earlier) the help of the garden architect, J.B. Papworth, who, towards the end of his life lived at Little Paxton near St Neots, a village at no great distance. As tradition recounts, the third Lord Ongley created the garden for his Swiss mistress and it was "splendidly arranged in imitation of Swiss scenery" as reported in the Morning Post of 1832. Hillocks and interlaced ponds with the islands and their humped bridges may have been formed on land which had previously been used for brickworks. The numerous buildings, cottages and the underground glass domed grotto were all erected at that time and flowering shrubs and covered walks added to the charm and romance of the garden.

A legend persists that the Swiss mistress sheltered from a thunderstorm under the large oak tree where she caught cold and died and was mourned by the poem 'The forgotten one' engraved on a marble open book in front of the tree. (The oak tree was given a thatched surrounding awning but sadly it later developed fungus and it had to be cut down during the recent restoration work). The legend cannot be corroborated as the poem which had become attributed to Lord Ongley was actually written by Letitia Landon and published in 1835 after she had visited a family nearby where a child had drowned. The legend further recounts that the Swiss girl had a child which died and is buried in the north-east corner of the garden. There are also stories of apparitions seen in the garden and later Dorothy asked an exorcist to come and lay the ghosts. The exorcist claimed that she saw a phantom of a young woman approach Dorothy and she now seemed quite happy as the stone cross marking the grave of her child had been returned to its original position after apparently having been moved by workmen.

Closer to the House, a Summer House was built on the north lawn near a large cedar tree. It must have been put up when Richard was still a baby as there is an unsigned design dated 1910. The rectangular pond and sunken garden were added a few years later, giving a more pleasant place to sit and enjoy the surrounding garden than the formal garden to the west of the house. The Summer House is a thatched pavilion with sliding doors to the veranda and it was furnished with cane furniture painted blue and with deck chairs. There were flower beds around

Fernery in the Grotto in the Swiss Garden

the pond and lavender bushes and roses and a sweet chestnut tree grew close by. Once one of Dorothy's dogs fell into the pond and drowned, being unable to clamber out so she had a mound of stones built at one end so that, should any other dog fall in, it should be able to climb out to save itself.

A large house of this size needed numerous servants to keep it running smoothly, like clockwork. For the surrounding gardens and the attached stables with the bothy, numerous outdoor workmen were also employed. When Frank married Dorothy in 1902, there were about a dozen servants running the House, now sometimes referred to as 'the mansion' and there were coachmen, grooms and gardeners apart from the estate staff under the agent, amongst whom were also numerous keepers and groundwork men. The hierarchy in a large country house was strictly adhered to and was ruled over by the housekeeper, at that time Mrs Waby who had moved to Old Warden as had the butler John Bardsley Hunt, both of whom had already worked for the Shuttleworths at Hartsholme Hall in Lincoln and then moved with Joseph and his second and much younger wife, Caroline Jane, to the new house at Old Warden Park. Both these two leading and highly valued servants were buried at the churchyard of St Leonard's near the Shuttleworth vault to show the esteem in which they had been held. The next

The Summer House at Old Warden Park, after 1915

Dolphin Tazza in front of Swiss Cottage in the Swiss Garden

Indian Kiosk in the Swiss Garden

butler, Everett, who, apart from his usual duties, taught both Dorothy's children, Richard and Anne, how to properly polish shoes as well as how to clean the silver. He always made the salad dressing in the dining room. wiping the bowl with a garlic clove and then adding cream and vinegar, Dorothy, my grandmother, continued to use his recipe for the rest of her life. Everett had come to Old Warden having worked for Alfred Shuttleworth in Lincoln as a valet first and then took over as butler when Bardsley Hunt retired and then he retired too in 1932 but was present at my mother, Anne's wedding in 1938, when he apparently affectionately handed her into the car after the reception. Everett was succeeded by the butler Roy. Mrs Fanny Cave was the cook and lived to be 86. She came from Rutland and also attended my mother's wedding but had retired by the year 1939. The valet was another important and confidential position and the Shuttleworths took the valet, Stapleton, with them on their trip around the world in 1906, sending him back with some of the excess baggage from the far east. Unfortunately, he had packed all Frank's right shoes in one trunk and the left shoes in another and one trunk went back to England whilst the other accompanied them for the rest of the journey with just shoes for one foot. The lady's maid was also a very personal and confidential position who together with the butler and housekeeper was closely involved in the lives of the master and mistress of the house.

After the middle of the last century, the life style changed out of all recognition for those who had lived and grown up in the previous times, both for the owners and for the employees. The greatest changes and then the only way to keep a grand house functioning were in some ways partly due to the invention and development of household equipment from Hoovers to washing machines to dish washers to today's dream possibility of turning on all needed equipment digitally and from any distance from a mobile phone or tablet. Staff were also being recruited in the 1950s from other countries and two young boys from St Helena were employed for the house, one who was called Cyril became an all-round house servant, learning to serve at table and finally to drive my grandmother locally if the chauffeur was not available. Cyril stayed on at Old Warden after Dorothy died and became an invaluable figure for the running of the house, his memories of events and general life in those years seen through the eyes of a boy of 16 arriving from the island of St Helena to a modern England in the early 1960s must have been astonishing. Now fifty years on, he too has reached retirement age and enjoys recounting his memories of Dorothy as a very old lady and Old Warden without him has become unthinkable.

Returning to the early years of the last century when Mrs Waby was the housekeeper, local history recounts her being very strict. The young girls working as housemaids, kitchen and scullery maids were ruled with a strong hand and, when marching them to church on a Sunday morning, she believed she must protect them from the curious and prying eyes of village boys. The young men employed as footmen, or hall boys were under the butler's supervision. Mrs Cave (mentioned above) was a much admired and respected cook, under whom the kitchen staff were employed. Each servant had individual responsibilities and the bells had to be answered when rung for help or attention.

Fires were to be laid and lit, the grates to be cleaned and polished, the furniture to be dusted and polished, the floors to be brushed or vacuumed and polished, the carpets to be brushed and beaten, all the picture frames, the mouldings, the ornaments to be dusted and the beds to be made as well as the wash basins filled with fresh water daily carried up from downstairs as no bathrooms had been installed when the house was built. There were two bathrooms on the second floor for bachelor guests created sometime later but, having a hip bath in front of a brightly burning fire, with hot water carried up in brass cans was still considered a greater luxury than having a bathroom with running hot and cold water.

A further bathroom was installed on the second floor when the nursery was prepared before the birth of Richard and any further children. Then Richard finally had a bathroom built for his mother when he came of age in 1932. This was installed in a partitioned off part of her bedroom, to be entered through a cupboard door. Downstairs the silver was kept in the safe next to the pantry and had to be polished and checked after every use under the supervision of the butler. The laundry was done at Laundry Farm in the village where a further group of employees worked, washing, starching and ironing all the tablecloths, napkins, staff's aprons, the clothes of the family and their children and the uniform of the servants, as well as the dust sheets used to cover furniture when the family was away, not to talk of drying cloths, dusters and floor cloths, and whatever else was needed in a large house.

In the House, flowers were to be arranged and vases placed in all the reception rooms, as well as in the guest rooms, decorations were to be made for the dining table. The flower arrangements were usually done by a gardener. One gardener, called Victor, was very gifted so was sent to Constance Spry after the second World War to do a special course in flower arranging. At the beginning of the twentieth century, the newspapers reported on the beauty and variety of bouquets made by the then head gardener, Mr. Modral, at the time of the Shuttleworths' wedding. He was succeeded by Frank Copcutt who had come from Waddesdon Manor, the Rothschilds' house in Buckinghamshire, where his father had been the head gardener. Copcutt was still head gardener at Old Warden in my childhood but he moved after the war to be head gardener for the Astors at Clivedon. His small son, Michael, was of the same age as I and we used to play together on my visits to Old Warden. The Copcutts lived in a small cottage at the east end of the kitchen gardens where a range of glass houses and potting sheds separated the eighteenth century walled garden from the out houses and the open parts of the garden. His successor was Childs who remained for many years during the period of change from a privately-run garden to being an institution with other priorities in gardening. Fruit and vegetables were grown in the kitchen gardens and were delivered to the kitchen every day and milk, butter and cream also came daily from the Home Farm. To the east, lay the 'marble bath' an abandoned feature from the old eighteenth-century manor house where the first snowdrops could always be found. A path winding on past the large pond led on through a shrubbery and down through an underpass with cobbled stones to the lake with its boat house and then continued to the main entrance to the Swiss Garden. This was enclosed by a wrought iron fence with elaborate gates, purported to have been made by the blacksmith Hart from Ickwell who had a smithy in the village outside the main gates to Old Warden Park. A not tenable legend persisted for many years that he was the uncle of Emma Hart, the famous beauty who became Lady Hamilton and was painted by the leading artists of her day (a painting of her hangs in the Dining room) but she actually had died many years before the Swiss Garden was even laid out.

In the stable yard were both the stables and the carriage houses which then became the garages after the advent of cars and, above them were flats for some of the grooms and other outdoor staff. The Head Groom was a Mr William Foster who lived down at Lakeside cottage on the north side of the lake, until he died in 1936. The first chauffeur was a Mr Norris, who remained for many years, well up into the 30s, and in 1934 Charles Edward Clarke, a very good looking and elegant man, came and remained until the late 1950s. He had been in the Royal Flying Corps during the first war, whilst his wife had been in service with Captain Arkwright of Harrold Hall who was the MFH of the Oakley, the local Hunt. The Clarkes lived in the village on Bedford Road and he came up to the House every day and looked after the fleet of cars and drove Dorothy when she went to London both before and after the second World War. He even gave me my first driving lessons in 1957.

Home Farm, originally called Park Farm, is just a short way down the back drive leading to Kingshill Farm and then on to the main road to Shefford. It supplied the house with all dairy products so, in due course. it came to be referred to as the "Home" Farm. There was a prize-winning herd of Guernsey cattle of which Dorothy was very proud. Their milk was deliciously creamy and the butter churned there a bright yellow – from the cows eating buttercups I was told as a child. The dairy was exceedingly clean, the cows always being washed or wiped down before milking and beside the milking parlour was the cooling room where butter and cream were made. Very often Dorothy used to take me there as a small child or sent me walking down with my nursemaid. There were of course, barns and sheds for the machinery and the other animals and the farm manager's house was also at the farm, as well as two small cottages.

There was also a Victorian stone house for the agent with a nice garden surrounding it built about the same time as the big house. Now new large hangars have been built beside the farm allowing the owners of private small planes to garage them there. The veteran cars with their workshop have also moved there from the Collection which is only a few hundred yards up the runway from the farm. Kingshill, the next farm down the back drive, was tenanted out to a farming family, the Capons, who still farm some of the land and take part of the estate shoot, also being the tenants of Manor Farm at Broom a few miles to the south. It is now planned that Kingshill Farm will be developed to be the centre of farming for the College, some buildings being restored with new appropriate buildings being built for animals, machinery, and storage.

Chapter 6

Frank and Dorothy: the newly wed couple

The years following the change wrought in Dorothy's life by her marriage were at first a continuous series of society gatherings interspersed by Frank's business meetings, by shoots and weekend house parties held at Old Warden or staying with friends as well as the annual Cowes Regatta week in early August. It must have been an overwhelming situation in which Dorothy found herself and I think she can be greatly admired for coping with the new world into which she had suddenly been propelled. As we have seen, her husband moved within the international society that travelled from one location to another, comparable to what we now refer to as the 'jet set' and Frank seems to have known 'anyone who was somebody' whether it be via his business contacts, his years in the Hussars, or his sporting activities, be it riding, coaching, shooting or sailing. He was firmly based within English society. For him it must have been a great delight to present his young and very attractive wife to the world at large. He took her with him to all society gatherings and ensured that she was presented at court so that she was eligible to attend any function where a member of the royal family was to be present. Dorothy was presented at court to King Edward VII and Queen Alexandra, probably in the spring of 1903. She wore a long dress with a train of yellow satin with silver Tudor roses, the material having been especially woven in Lyon, and wore the tiara of pearls above diamond crescents that Frank had given her for Christmas; she told me how she found it in the Christmas stocking lying on her bed on her first married Christmas morning. I later turned the yellow satin train into an evening dress which I wore at many balls and occasions in the early 1960s, and which I have now donated to the Textile Department of the Landesmuseum in Stuttgart.

Dorothy Clotilda Shuttleworth dressed as Anne Boleyn for Masque in 1906

Dorothy dressed for Presentation at Court 1903

Having rented a house in Berkeley Square enabled the Shuttleworths to attend London functions as well as entertain at Old Warden and take part in other shooting parties held at the houses of their friends. In London, the season started in the spring after the presentation parties and, apart from private balls, there were many charitable functions to be attended given in support of some worthy organisation. Tableaux vivants were popular at that time by which the participants were clad as historical figures and arranged in a set grouping of some important episode from history, or people took part in masques, again dressed as historical figures or characters from literature. Frank and Dorothy appeared at many of these balls. Once she was dressed as Anne Boleyn in a beautiful blue velvet gown with a ruff and matching hat whilst Frank was dressed as Sir Walter Raleigh, both performing in the Masque of Life at Claremont House in July 1907. Frank also made sure that Dorothy was painted by some of the leading artists of the day. In 1904, having appeared at a fancy-dress dance clad as 'The Parson's Daughter' a painting by Romney exhibited at the Tate, wearing the costume of the period and with a chestnut or auburn coloured wig, she was then portrayed by Dicksee wearing the dress but with her own auburn hair, painted in profile, setting a bowl

Dorothy Clotilda Shuttleworth
miniature c.1903

Dorothy as 'The Parson's Daughter'
Frank Dicksee 1905

of flowers with anemones. The painting was shown at the Royal Academy in 1905 and today still hangs in the house dining room at Old Warden. Dicksee painted her again in 1912, with her 3-year-old son standing on a sofa beside her and Francois Flameng painted a wonderfully flamboyant full-length portrait of her holding in her arms a Chin puppy-dog (one of those which had been bought in Japan on their world trip of 1906) and the clock tower of Old Warden is visible in the background. The artist charged sixteen hundred pounds which included the portrait's very ornate baroque carved and gilt frame. Another charity ball in June 1912 called the Hundred Years Ball, took place at the Royal Albert Hall in London, at which Dorothy was dressed as an officer of the Spanish dragoons. A press photograph shows her amongst a group of seven society ladies, all in appropriate costumes. The Albert Hall was lavishly decorated to look like the Brighton Pavilion at the time of George IV. The ball was held during the official court mourning for King Edward VII but, as it was a charity event, even all members of the Royal Family who attended wore full evening dress and jewels.

Visits to the opera at Covent Garden were a regular occurrence, when white tie and tails were worn by the gentlemen and the ladies wore evening dress and, if they were married, a tiara. As mentioned above, after the death of King Edward VII in 1912, court mourning was declared and when, during that time Dorothy went to the opera, she would wear a tiara made of jet, of which she had two, one of a classical Greek key pattern and the other a more delicate pointed model. Dorothy told me about how when George Bernard Shaw's play "Pygmalion" was first performed in London, the renowned actress, Mrs Patrick Campbell, had the role of Eliza Doolittle and everyone in London wanted to hear her say "Not bloody likely" still then considered a very scandalous expression.

Trips to Paris must have been made regularly as Dorothy attended fashion shows buying at Molyneux and at Worth and she chose a scent, Mitsouko made by Guerlain, that she wore for the rest of her life.

Most years there were three shooting weekends at Old Warden, where the shoot had an excellent reputation and had grown into a famous pheasant and partridge shoot, the bag being in the direction of 1200 to 1300 pheasants and partridges. The guest book also includes the card with the 'bag' of the day and a group photograph was often taken on the steps of the front door porch. Amongst the guests were many figures from English society. Lord Scarborough came regularly as did the Curzons, the Lords Wemyss, Willoughby, Royston, the Grevilles, the Ellisons, the Duke of Warwick, the Listowels and many neighbours such as the Whitbreads, the Pyms, the Ormsby-Gores, Osbornes, Comptons and the Diggles too who were close friends for many years having shared interests in sailing, then Lord Tweeddale, Lord Ormonde, the Duke of Somerset, Mrs Kepple and the Colvilles to name just a few of those signing the guest books. William McClaren Campbell, later to be Dorothy's second husband. also appears in the guest books as attending a shoot as well being on board the yacht. There were also international friends who came over from Paris and elsewhere such as the Clarys, the Counts Bathyanys and Andrassys from Hungary, the Pierpont Morgans and Count Blücher and the Schröders, as well as the Euphrussis from Paris, now so well known since the book 'The Hare with Amber Eyes' written a few years ago by the nephew, Edmund de Waal.

Alongside all these social activities, both Frank and Dorothy were actively involved in the life of Old Warden, of the villagers and the tenants. There were annual tea parties for the tenants and the inmates of the Biggleswade workhouse were invited for an afternoon. In 1903 The Rev. Cassels was appointed vicar to succeed the Rev. Hodgson who had unexpectedly died. In June 1905, a Bishop

Cottage in the village of Old Warden

Old Warden village street scene, on left is the Reading room,
and on the right is the Hare & Hounds public house

Cassels dedicated a stained-glass window in the church donated by Dorothy. A constitutional fete was held in the park for the Beds and North Beds Unionists in July 1903, prizes being distributed by the Member of Parliament, Lord Compton. In 1903 Frank had the Reading and Recreation Room built for the village, the management of which was left to the members although Frank was the first chairman, making a donation to set it up, whilst the gardener, Mr Modral, became the secretary and treasurer of the committee. There were two billiard tables and card tables for playing whist and cribbage, as well as dominoes or draughts. In the next room, daily papers were laid out on the reading table as well as various periodicals. The members were the men and youths of the village who also partook in smoking concerts and whist and billiard handicaps with a small annual membership fee being charged.

The village of Old Warden was recommended in the press of that year 1903 as being a model village, with an annual cottage garden competition for which prizes were awarded by Col Shuttleworth, points being given for the cleanliness of the gardens, the rotation of crops and the general appearance of the village. This competition continued during the twenties and thirties but probably stopped due to the Second World War. A few years later, it was reported in the Daily Mirror that the village 'now almost forgotten' was a pioneer of 'garden cities' and was visited by a group of delegates interested in housing reform. Rents were then remarkably low and an equipped cottage with garden could be rented for one shilling a week. What is not mentioned is that sanitation was far from being desirable, baths and other amenities did not exist. There was a bathhouse but proper plumbing was only installed in every cottage towards the end of the last century! One hundred years previously, towards the end of the nineteenth century, some cases of typhoid erupted, probably due to the village water pumps becoming infected, so that the school had to be closed on various occasions and a few deaths were lamented and recorded. In recent years, a few of the cottages as well as the pub have been sold but the majority remain the property of the Trust and the County planning authorities do not encourage new buildings to be added to the village, which helps to maintain the charm of the time it was built but rather limits the possible developments of any further housing required.

Nearby, on land that was originally part of Warden Monastery, a Tudor manor house still partly stands, the land now belonging to the Southill estate. Recently it has been restored by the Landmark Trust, and is one of their premises to be let as is the folly, part of the Shuttleworth estate, on the crest of the Warren known as

Dorothy dressed in riding attire for Hunt c.1905

Queen Anne's Summerhouse, presumably built when Samuel Ongley was knighted by Queen Anne in 1712 and radiating avenues lead from there. It is aligned to the south with a small classical temple on the lake at Southill and to the north via an avenue leading to Old Warden House. The folly, which was lived in during the nineteenth century by the Ongley's gamekeeper, Stonebridge, with numerous children, has now, together with the keeper's cottage just a short distance away and built later by the Shuttleworths, been beautifully restored by the Landmark Trust and once again Queen Anne's Summerhouse stands as a genuine landmark on the crest of the Warren. Possibly in the days of Warden Abbey, a monk may have lived in a hermitage in the same position to watch over the rabbits kept for feeding the monks.

In 1905 when Frank turned 60, he resigned from being Master of the Cambridgeshire Foxhounds but continued to hunt, as did Dorothy who rode daily right up to the second World War, always riding side saddle as mentioned before. Various reports are to be found about Frank retiring from some positions he held.

Queen Anne Cottage in the Warren c.1920

He had already retired from the Yeomanry in 1903, being allowed to retain his rank and to continue to wear the uniform, then from the Hunt. Newspaper cuttings mention that the couple were 'living a more quiet life in their beautiful Bedfordshire country house and not entertaining as much as previously', which could seem to insinuate that Frank's health was not very good. All the same, a cruise of the Mediterranean on the yacht of two months duration was reported for that year and probably the trip around the world was being planned. This was to take place in 1906, just after the Russo-Japanese War of 1904 had ended, in the aftermath of which the British Monarch was to give the Emperor of Japan the Order of the Garter and this leads on to the story of the Shuttleworths' trip around the World.

Chapter 7

The World Tour of 1906

Dorothy wrote a diary of about forty pages in all, describing the daily events of the whole tour and began compiling a large and very heavy leather-bound album which was signed by their friends and other passengers. The diary describes her view of life then so well and the accompanying photos, partly taken by her or acquired on the trip, together with postcards of some of the places they visited, is a fascinating record. As well as signatures of their friends, the album has decorative drawings and small sketches augmenting the photographs. Not only are they a record of the voyage, but also a lesson in the manners of the time - never is anyone referred to by their Christian name, they are always given their full name, be it a title, army rank, or Mr and Mrs. I am therefore unsure whether many of those referred to were friends before they departed and had possibly even planned the voyage with them, or were only met during the trip and became friends as they shared many experiences.

The Shuttleworths must have had contacts all around the world, not only the official agents and emissaries in the countries they visited. They were often given special treatment and, before sailing on to Canada where they were wined and dined both there and then in New York, help was continually offered. I presume that Frank's business links were very wide and well developed so that people or acquaintances were always pleased to meet and entertain them. I am not aware whether any new business contacts were made for the company but certainly the social contacts they developed on the trip gave them an enlarged circle of friends who were afterwards often invited either to Old Warden or to a visit on the yacht or met again in London or Paris. As the diary is the only remaining document hand written by Dorothy, I am reporting in quite some length about the journey.

SS Mongolia: from Tilbury Docks to Colombo

Frank and Dorothy departed on the S.S. Mongolia from Tilbury Docks, on the morning of the 5th January 1906. The Mongolia was a P&O 10,000-ton steam ship and a postcard shows it rolling in heavy seas. The first few days were very rough as they steamed through the Bay of Biscay and, only after they passed Gibraltar, did it become calmer and warmer. At Marseille, the "Garter Party" came on board. King Edward VII was sending his young nephew, Prince Arthur of Connaught, on an official state visit to present the Order of the Garter to the Emperor of Japan for having fought in 1904 with the English in the battle at Port Arthur against the Russians. Prince Arthur was accompanied by Lord Redesdale, General Thomas Kelly-Kenny, Sir Edward Seymour, Col. Arthur Davidson and his secretary, Lampson.

The Shuttleworths went ashore at Marseille, and drove around the harbour and the town but found chaos when they returned to the ship which very crowded and some people had mislaid their luggage. The dining saloon was full of many elegant ladies heading for Cairo. They then sat at the Captain's table next to the table of Prince Arthur. Dorothy wrote about the beauty of the coast and the many islands. They saw Stromboli by moon light and a burst of flame issuing from the volcano. They continued through the Mediterranean, sailed through the Suez Canal and called in at Aden.

Statue of De Lesseps (who built the Suez Canal) at Port Said

Colombo Harbour and landing Jetty

Ceylon

They continued to Ceylon where they interrupted the journey to visit the island and landed at Colombo where unfortunately an acquaintance from Colworth House in Bedfordshire, also travelling on the ship with his wife and daughter, was taken ill and then tragically died. They went inland by train and went to the top of Mount Pedro from where there was a splendid view and travelled for a few days around the island with some friends also on the ship, noting the wonderful vegetation and meeting some of the planters living there. The Shuttleworths then boarded another ship called the Delta of only 8000 tons which they found more comfortable and had two cabins opposite each other and also sat at the Captain's table. A group of about a dozen friends signed the album around a picture of the ship. Among the ship's passengers with whom they were acquainted were the Earl and Countess of Leitrim (later Countess Violet was to become godmother to the Shuttleworth's only son, Richard, born in 1909), an American couple J. Low Harriman and his wife Elizabeth, a railway heiress, and a French landowner, Comte Guillaume de Ganay and his friend, Monsieur E. Schneider. The Shuttleworths travelled parts of the journey in company with some of these friends or met them again at different places.

View of top of Mt Pedro

Singapore and Hong Kong

After arriving at Singapore, they and their valet, Stapleton, were vaccinated before continuing to Hong Kong as cases of smallpox had been discovered amongst the crew. They went to lunch at Raffles, the famous hotel, and drove to see the Botanical Gardens. Dorothy often notes that Frank was not well and had to spend a day in bed but they were able to celebrate his sixty first birthday on 16th February with a tea party on board and she gave him a tie she had crocheted.

View of Hong Kong, 1906

China

In Shanghai, they stayed in a hotel and booked the next passage. Dorothy employed a Chinese maid to accompany her for part of the trip. She couldn't manage the Chinese name so called her Cecile but sacked her again a short time later. Here they went shopping, buying silk and some jade rings as presents to take home. They arrived at Hong Kong on 23rd February where they went ashore to book the next stage of the journey and were delighted with the town, doing a tour in a rickshaw through Chinatown and were very impressed by the beautiful harbour.

The next few days were cold and very foggy. When they arrived at Hoosung, they transferred to a P&O tender to take them two hours upstream to Shanghai, where they stayed at the Astor House Hotel and had a roaring fire lit to get warm. They were invited to a dance by the General Manager of the Shanghai Bank who had been on the Delta with them. They did a certain amount of shopping, going to a leading silk manufacturer, and Frank had his hair cut. Together with the Harrimans, they visited the American Consul who assured them that it was safe to go to Peking, despite some missionaries having been murdered a short time previously. They then changed their plans to go together with the Harrimans

Great Wall of China, 1906

by land as there was much ice reported on the water route, so followed hectic re-packing and changing of tickets. All the same, they first of all continued on a boat up the Yangtse to Hangkow, stopped at the port of Nanking which is some distance from the town and were astonished to see thousands of ducks on the river. They then went ashore at Wu-Hu and went to the Roman Catholic church where their friend, Mme Schneider, prayed whilst they were followed by a crowd of a few thousand which frightened Dorothy, knowing that a massacre of missionaries had taken place there in 1891. Desert sand prevented the boat continuing as it was as thick as fog so they then only arrived at Hankow the next day having passed through the lake of Poyang, closer to where the latest murder of missionaries had taken place. After a night in the Terminus hotel, the following day they boarded a train and had two carriages for the group and had to take a cook with them. Dorothy found it all quite fun but rough, as the journey took four days passing through flat country to begin with and then it became hilly where they saw the Wall of China and many small villages. The train had to stop at night as the track had only been open for three months but in future trains would be able to continue during the night as new Pullmans were on order which would reduce the journey to 36 hours instead of four days as it then was.

They crossed the Yellow River on a new but rickety bridge still being built, and stopped for the night again at Sin-siang-cien, where they went to see the house of an English engineer working there and visited some old temples. The last day from Shun-Te-Fou to Peking, which they reached in mid-March, the train passed walled cities through a very dusty region. In Peking, they stayed at a Hotel of the Wagon-Lits and found that the other friends had arrived before them. The next days they visited Peking and the Summer Palace. Dorothy's uncle, General Sir Hope-Grant, had captured the Summer Palace in 1860 and Dorothy had inherited a small famille-verte porcelain bowl which originated from there, despite the fact that the General had forbidden his troops to loot. They visited an old friend of his, Sir Robert Hart, who despite introductions gave them a cool reception and they then tried to call on the Minister who was not at home.

Dorothy then developed a nasty bout of influenza and was not well for about five days during which time Frank and their friends visited various of the sights but she was able to join them for the last day and visited the Tartar City and the Temple of Heaven which she described as beautiful but, in general, Dorothy had not appreciated what she saw of China and found it very dusty. She wrote that they saw many graves which had opened due to floods. Mme Schneider had been to see the Ming tombs which had taken her two days.

When they finally left Peking, they went by train to Tientsin which was very dusty but it had become warmer. They stayed at the Astor House Hotel where they re-joined their other friends, the Phillips, who were waiting for a boat which they discovered was to leave two days later from Tangku to where they caught the next train. There they stayed in 'a fearful little pot house' (the Station Hotel) where they all had to sleep sharing beds and all wrapped up to keep warm, until they were woken at 5a.m. to catch the boat – a launch. It was delayed for nearly the whole day and then ran aground and had to wait for the water to rise. Frank now had a bad cold and Dorothy reported they stayed in a tiny filthy cabin with hardly any air and the launch was full of German and Italian passengers. They then finally had a difficult transfer to the Takeshima Maru where there were six first class cabins and a small dining saloon. The boat could not sail that night and a rat which ran over one of the guests' face caused a huge hullabaloo and frightened them all. Frank looked around for the rat the next day when the ship was still loading cargo and did not sail until the following day after another night with a rat scare. It was again bitterly cold and even snowed so the ship had turned up the hot steam pipes so much that Dorothy then complained it was like a Turkish bath.

Japan

They went ashore in the launch of the customs officer at Chefoo where they found the scenery attractive but the port dilapidated and sent a wire to the Wilsons in Tokyo explaining their delay. They passed close to the Korean coast and finally anchored at Nagasaki the evening of the following day, 25th March. Dorothy found the harbour the most beautiful she had ever seen with magnificent scenery. The boat continued to Moji where a doctor came to inspect them. The ship had been used as a hospital ship during the recent war and was now on its first civilian trip, very comfortable with about 30 passengers. The captain reported that the coast was still heavily mined and that a Chinese junk had been blown up a short while before.

When they arrived at Kobe. they decided to go to Kyoto by train to meet the Wilsons but missed them and so returned to Kobe to be on board for dinner. They then planned to take all their baggage with them the following day by train to stay at the Yaamai Hotel in the hills above Kyoto where the Wilsons and the Leitrims were staying. They had a veranda around their apartment in the hotel and were surprised when the guide walked straight in the next morning. He was called Kosaka and spoke very good English and he was to accompany them for the duration of their stay in Japan.

The Shuttleworths were to spend nearly a month in Japan. It was April, the time of the cherry blossom, with many festivals. They were enchanted by everything they saw and started buying Japanese treasures which were readily available at that time. Japan had been closed to the rest of the world for over two centuries and now it had become a most popular country to visit with much influence on the development of some of the contemporary artists of the western world. The feudal system had been abolished some years previously and many of the old feudal lords had lost their influence and their position in Japanese society so that more than a few of them were also forced to sell their treasures. Some dealers pretended to have old inheritances which they were selling, having fallen on hard times and the wealthy tourists were easy game! Frank and Dorothy started on a real shopping spree, buying lacquer work, netsuke and a big temple gong as well as trinkets galore. Their guide, Kosaka, took them to some of the most successful dealers amongst whom was Thomas Blow from Welwyn in Hertfordshire, who had originally been a bee specialist and a botanist. He had visited Japan first in 1896 collecting samples of plants and wrote a report on Beekeeping for the Japanese Ministry of Agriculture. He had then married a Japanese lady in London and was residing in Kyoto by 1904, owning the first automobile in that city and where he remained until the outbreak of World War I. The Shuttleworths went to the Blows' house which Dorothy describes in her diary as having paper windows and sliding doors and they had to sit on the floor whilst they were entertained to tea. Mrs Blow impressively owned over one hundred dresses and beautiful kimonos. They then bought a set of hand painted china and some cloisonné boxes, only later realising that Blow was a dealer who was, as Dorothy said, 'posing as a gentleman'!

One day they took a train to Hozu and came back by boat down the rapids. Another day they went to the lake of Biwa which is thirty-six miles long and saw the ancient pine tree supported by props, before visiting the temple of Onjo-ji, also known as Mi-dera, and saw the famous bell near Otsu. They returned by boat along a canal and through many tunnels of nearly two miles in length in total darkness. They went to a cherry blossom dance where geishas sang and danced and 'squeaked and mewed like cats'. They continued their souvenir acquisition, buying presents for all family members and pieces for themselves. They were given permits to visit the Emperor's palace built fifty years before and then fell in love with the Chin, Japanese dogs similar in size to a King Charles spaniel. They moved on to Tokyo by train and, whilst waiting for their room in the hotel, witnessed an earthquake which terrified Dorothy. They called on the British Embassy and, at Ikedas bought 16 pieces of porcelain and they were invited to a geisha dance at Kosaka's brother's house.

They then decided to buy four Chin at a dog shop and wired to Kyoto to also buy Mitsu, a puppy that they had first seen there. After driving through a two-and-a-half-mile long cherry avenue, they dined at the Embassy with the very first British ambassador to Japan, Sir Claude MacDonald and his wife, Lady MacDonald.

Frank Shuttleworth with Japanese Chin dogs on board ship returning from world trip 1906

The next place they visited was Nikko where they rode up the eight mile long trip through cryptomeria avenues and wild scenery

Shinto Temple at Nikko, 1906

Carving at Nikko:
"hear no evil, speak no evil, see no evil"

to the lake at Chuzenji and, on Easter Sunday, 15th April they went to visit the temple at Ieyasu where they saw the famous carving Dorothy always referred to all her life - the three monkeys: 'hear no evil, speak no evil and see no evil' which is on a lintel leading into the temple above the grave of the 2nd Shogun, and then also saw the sacred horse of the Bishop of Nikko.

Again, they shopped before leaving by train for Imaichi and they then heard that the hotel they had stayed at in Kyoto had burned down and guests had lost everything. In Tokyo, they went to a garden party given by the Ambassador in Baron Iwasaki's garden and then next day, arrayed in their best, they set off in a rather ramshackle carriage for the reception held in a beautiful garden with double cherry trees where they had been invited by the Emperor Meiji and his Empress who wore European clothes, she dressed in mauve. They saw some of the most prominent politicians and generals, among whom were General Nogi and Admiral Togo who had taken Port Arthur during the Russo-Japanese war in 1905.

Later that day they heard that there had been a fearful earthquake in San Francisco (where they had been planning to sail to after leaving Japan) with the whole city on fire. Dorothy later told me that the dogs had been very unsettled the previous day and she had been told by locals that that could be a sign of an imminent earthquake. In fact, that earthquake had been felt by dogs all around the Pacific Rim.

Before their final departure and after last purchases of Japanese treasures, they were invited to the house of their guide, Kosaka, to watch a lesson given by a professor in Ikebana flower arranging. They were introduced to Kosaka's mother and to his bride of only nineteen, to whom they gave a coral brooch and they were very impressed by Kosaka's collection, amongst which was the best white jade bowl they had yet seen, as well as a lot of lacquer work. Later they were to hear that he had been murdered by another guide.

For a final trip, they went by train and by rickshaw through beautiful scenery in the mountains to the best hotel they had yet seen - the Fujiya and continued to the lake of Hakone the next day but, as it was misty and the clouds were so low, they were unable to see Mount Fuji. They were joined there by some of the American friends they had been travelling with earlier.

The next day they went via Kozu by train to Kamakura to see the forty-nine foot high bronze statue of Buddha made 600 years ago which one could go inside of and then a wooden forty-foot sculpture of a goddess of mercy in the temple of Kannon and then back to Tokyo by train where they were invited to stay the last night in the private house of their guide, sleeping in the main room on a silk mattress and they dined together seated on the floor. Before catching the train to Yokohama, they lunched at the Imperial Hotel after seeing the damage the fire had caused in the town the day before. Dorothy had left her camera somewhere on the trip the previous day but it was returned to her as they went to the train station. Dorothy had become very adept with her Kodak Brownie which had only been invented in 1900 and she continued to use it for many years.

At Yokohama, they had to get certificates for the Chin dogs from the American health officer at the Consulate. Again, they went to a curio shop and bought a stand and some irons. She also bought some Japanese fairy tales before walking to the quay to see the ship, the Hakuai Maru, where they left cards for the captain. They had to stay at the Club Hotel as the better ones were full up and the next morning Kosaka arrived with the dogs which were given a large room outside the hotel. A visit to a nursery garden was followed by calling on the British Consul and then another visit to Samurai Shoku and to a friend of Kosaka's who once again had 'fallen on bad times' and where they bought a large bell gong and a lacquer and ivory box as well as a sword.

The next morning, the 27th April, the Shuttleworths boarded the Empress of India, a 6000-ton steam ship, where they had a nice cabin although the ship was very full but the dogs were able to be installed in a nice warm place near the vegetable cupboard. Mme Schneider was also on board with her daughter who was unwell, as well as Mrs Wood whom they had met before. They were on board for ten days before reaching Victoria and the ship rolled and pitched very unpleasantly nearly all the way. It was generally uncomfortable and dirty with cockroaches and the food 'shocking'. The weather was cold and even snowing, although by now it was the end of April. Every day they walked the dogs on deck and played with them as well as listening to concerts in the evening and joining in sports on the decks, until they finally arrived at Victoria early in the morning and steamed on to reach Vancouver by 2pm, reporting a lovely harbour entrance but passing some burnt woods on the way there.

SS Empress of India: from Japan to Vancouver

Canada and America

Upon landing, they first rushed to the Canadian Pacific Railway office to see about their reservations, but were kept hanging around for over an hour and told to return later as there were only three men dealing with the passengers off two steamers. They finally found the baggage agent who was helpful about the dogs and then, taking Mrs Wood with them, took a carriage and drove about 9 miles to Stanley Park which was like a forest with its impressive trees. However, they found the town of Vancouver unattractive with high rise buildings and trams. They had tea and collected their tickets for the train having sent their luggage in bond ahead to New York and then returned to spend the night on the ship.

The train left the following morning at an early hour. They were not pleased with their carriage but enjoyed the splendid scenery as they passed through the Fraser Canyon and travelled along the Thompson River. As the dogs were in the baggage wagon and the train stopped quite often, they were able to let the dogs out for short walks. The same train had been held up by bandits whilst coming west and a paper cutting about it is included in the album.

The scenery impressed them enormously and Dorothy stayed up until late since the countryside was illuminated by moonlight as they wound through the Rocky Mountains which were still covered in snow, sometimes with four engines pulling the train. She was up early next morning as they reached Field where she saw a bear – on a chain - and then on to Laggan where a dining car was finally attached.

At Banff, they saw Red Indians and their houses and reached Calgary at 2pm where they got out and bought a postcard (in the album). The land was flat like the downs with ranches dotted around as the train continued eastwards. The next morning, they stopped at Winnipeg where the station was still being built and were able to walk to the main street.

The following day, as they passed along Lake Superior, they caught up with the train from the previous day which had had to stop for a full 24 hours because a wooden bridge had been on fire and was damaged and so had had further to wait until it was repaired adequately for the trains to cross. There are many islands and the lake glittered in the sunshine so they walked about a while and took photos and then finally arrived three hours late at North Bay. Mrs Wood travelled on to Montreal but the Shuttleworths continued to Toronto where they stayed at the King Edward Hotel.

Niagara Falls, 1906

The following day, they took a train to Niagara where they hired a motor car and drove around seeing Goat Island and to both the American Falls and the Horseshoe and Canadian Falls and went under the Horseshoe Falls wearing oilskins and rubber boots and found it magnificent. They saw the whirlpool below the rapids where Captain Webb had been drowned trying to swim across, and were photographed by the man who had witnessed it and who had also taken a photograph of a forty-five-year-old American woman who had had herself rolled over the falls in a wooden barrel and was then unconscious for a fortnight but had survived. They hurried back but, not knowing the way, were given wrong directions and only arrived at the station as the third train pulled out, so took another train to see a different view of the falls which was lovely.

The river comes from the lakes, Superior, Erie, Huron and Michigan. Ontario, they had passed on the way from Toronto, so they finally returned to their hotel at 8.30 that evening. The next morning, they tried to buy collars for the little dogs but only found chains and then washed the dogs at the tailor's shop, having found the way directions were given most confusing, "When you are on King Street, turn north and then east, etc". They were collected by a Mrs McPherson and a

Miss Pattison in their motor car to go out to lunch with Mrs McGuiness at the Hunt Club which was seven miles away in a lovely park on cliffs overlooking Lake Ontario. There were seven ladies and Frank the only man. They returned by train accompanied by three of the ladies who wanted to see the dogs which they then took to a park to be walked.

Mr Blackstock, a K.C. who looked like one of Leach's paintings dined with them. The next day they were collected by Mr Pattison. the father of two of the ladies they had met the previous day, who drove them around Toronto to see the Parliament buildings and Colleges. They caught a late afternoon train to New York but were soon delayed as there had been a railroad accident so only arrived the next morning at 9a.m. on 17th May. The weather had turned lovely and very warm and the train ran along the Hudson River giving them a splendid view.

Frank and Dorothy checked in to the Waldorf Astoria Hotel and Dorothy writes that the rooms were similar to those they had in the Paris Ritz, but with a telephone. They were on the 6th floor but the hotel had 15 floors and they found a huge basket of American Beauty roses awaiting them from Mrs Sherrill with whom they dined that evening, together with Mrs Gibbs at 20 East 65th Street in a lovely house. Dorothy was impressed by the buildings and found it a beautiful city. Frank bought her a dress and a hat and they found collars for the dogs. The next day was extremely hot - 90° in the shade. They drove in an electric cab to Central Park but were not allowed to put the dogs down. They had tea at the Claremont Restaurant with a view over the Hudson River. She writes that the service in the hotel was not good and it was very expensive.

The following day they collected their tickets at the White Star Headquarters on Broadway and walked the dogs along the river bank. On Sunday, there was church with a long sermon and the next day they went with Mrs Gibbs in an electric landaulet to the downtown office of Mr Sherrill who took them to lunch at Delmonico's. Major Whitney was also present. The manager of the North American Bank took them up to the roof on the 26th floor looking over the Cannon Street, 'the closest to heaven' she had ever been, writes Dorothy, the people on the streets appearing like insects. Then they went to the Stock Exchange Gallery where a seat costs 18,000 pounds only granting the right to walk on the floor and grab a chair! They were all shouting but Mr Sherrill said it was a quiet day. The last day they ordered orchids to be sent to Mrs Sherrill and, after driving to the park and riverside, dined at Sherry's which was very full.

On May 23rd they drove to the Docks to see the ship – the Oceanic of 17,000 tons belonging to the White Star Line which they boarded in the early afternoon and had two cabins. A huge crowd came to see the ship off, amongst them many friends: Major Whitney who introduced them to his sister who was also on the ship, Mrs Gibbs brought them sweets and Mrs Sherrill brought cakes, as did Mrs Wood with her niece. It was a lovely evening as they sailed down the river past Long Island and Sandy Hook. Again. they sat at the Captain's table as did a Major FitzGerald and a Captain Battye. The Atlantic crossing took seven days and it was warm at first then much colder but they did not see any icebergs. The dogs were near the propeller room which was not nice and Mitsu was ill, as were some of the passengers.

The last evening there was a concert and an auction where Frank was the chairman and bid 6 pounds for an auction program with the signatures of all performers (in the album). A Mr Babbington had written a letter to help re importing the dogs. They finally passed Queenstown and then docked at Liverpool at 9a.m. on the morning of May 30th having been around the world in four and a half months.

Chapter 8

Life in Society and Family events

Once back in England, Frank and Dorothy started their social routine again, announcing their presence for the London season in the Press in the column of the Court Circular in the early summer of 1906: racing events, fashionable balls, the Four in Hand Club, business meetings and then boarding the yacht for the annual week at Cowes. The following winter some of the friends who also had been on the world trip came to Old Warden for a shoot in early 1907, the bag was 1,000 – 1,500 for six guns.

A year later, in March 1908, the Reverend Robert Lang (who had become rector of Woodham Walter in Essex) died and was buried at Old Warden. His son, Harold, who had been the assistant vicar, now took over the parish, and his widow, Adine, continued to live there with her son.

At the Cowes Regatta week in early August of that year, the Shuttleworths were on their yacht, the Mera, and as usual had many guests. A cruise to Holland via Dover then took place where a friend, Mary Searoyd, came on board for a week and Dorothy's youngest brother, Arthur, spent about a fortnight on board with them. Photos in the yachts' guest book show Dutch ports, a windmill and children dressed in local costume and wearing clogs.

In late September, Dorothy went to Bad Ems where she stayed at the Hotel Englischer Hof to do a cure. Bad Ems had been a well-known Spa since the Napoleonic times, famous for its salt springs, and gained notorious fame due to the so called 'Ems Dispatch' in 1870 when the Prussian King Wilhelm and his chancellor, Bismarck, sent a sharply worded refusal to the French request not to support the claim of a Hohenzollern nephew to the Spanish throne. This thereby

Frank's yacht SY 'Mera' RYS

prevented the French Emperor Napoleon III achieving a much-needed political victory in France which led to France declaring war on Prussia, relying on the support of Austria and Italy. This developed into the ignominious Franco-Prussian War of 1870 which ended in the capitulation of the French Emperor and the nomination of the Prussian King to be the Emperor of all Germany, this tactlessly being announced in the famous Gallerie des Glaces in the Palace of Versailles.

The Spa itself was mainly renowned for respiratory ailments but also, according to a medical report of the time, for nearly all complaints of any organs, as well as being beneficial for nervous strain. There was a famous spring known amongst the locals as the 'Buberlquelle' where by tradition women who were longing for a baby son and who drank from the spring's waters would have a son nine months later. Although Frank who seemed prone to bronchitis or similar illnesses does not seem to have been with her, Dorothy spent some weeks in Bad Ems and paid for treatment by the leading practitioner, Dr Vogler of third generation renown. She also seems to have been in contact with a Dr Hall who had a practice in London and also looked after patients in Bad Ems in the summer months.

Frank and Dorothy had been married for more than five years and they were presumably longing to have a son and heir. Frank was ailing somewhat and was already over sixty and Dorothy approaching thirty and, for those days, neither would have been considered young. Whether the salt waters of the famous spring helped or not, Dorothy did become pregnant that autumn, and the long-awaited son was born the following summer. Sir James and Lady Adams, great friends of Dorothy's, were said to be there at the same time. Whether they were friends from earlier times, or they met there, I do not know. The Adams were then still living in Scotland where he was a judge but a few years later, they moved south to Colne Park near Colchester, in Essex.

One of their daughters, Anne, was born the same year as Dorothy's son, Richard, and the Adams were regular visitors and later they often travelled together, one grandson becoming one of Dorothy's godchildren and today we, the descendants, are still good friends.

Birth of Richard

On 16th July 1909, the long-awaited son and heir was born at Old Warden and was christened Richard Ormonde at St Leonard's parish church a month later. The local press reports record the event in great detail. On 20th August, Richard was christened by his uncle, the Rev Harold Lang, assisted by the local parson, the Rev. G.K. Cassels. The organ was played by Mr Birch and the chosen hymns were "In Token Thou Shalt Not Fear" and "Fight the Good Fight." The church was decorated with flowers, again arranged by the head gardener, Modral. The chosen godparents were not all able to attend - the Marquis of Ormonde and Alfred Shuttleworth were present and then Lady Leitrim was represented by the grandmother, Adine Lang, and Lord Scarborough by Frank himself.

Afterwards there was a large lunch and tea party in a marquee in front of the house which was reached by the drive through the park. The main gates were decorated with a banner bearing the word WELCOME with a Union Jack flag and wreaths of flowers. The marquee had space for 600 guests and the catering was done by Messrs Dudeney and Johnson of Bedford, all the arrangements being made by the indomitable agent, Mr Munckton. The christening presents were displayed in front of the high table, amongst which were a gold goblet given by the tenants of the Old Warden and Broom Estates and another goblet with a spoon by the tenants of the Goldington Estate. The housekeeper, Mrs Waby, and the butler, John Bardsley Hunt, gave a silver mug and spoon and Nurse Joyce, Miss Garton and Mrs Larner gave a three-handled silver cup. There were further presents from tenants of Cople and Willington and from the employees of the Old Warden estate, as well as valuable gifts from the godparents, from the family and from close friends.

A toast was first drunk to the Royal family, proposed by the host and then a tenant, Mr Herbert King, proposed the health of the baby which he admitted to not having seen but was assured he would become a worthy successor to his father in due course. Frank thanked everyone eloquently and reminded those present that seven years ago to the day, he and his wife had celebrated the return from their honeymoon and now. despite the rain which prevented the baby being present, he felt assured that the friendship with the tenants and employees of the estate would continue in the same harmonious way. He also thanked all who had brought presents and particularly mentioned the silver mug given by two servants who had been with his family for 49 and 50 years of uninterrupted service - Mrs Waby and John Bardsley Hunt. He then proposed the health of the tenants and stressed the good relationship between all on the estate which was reciprocated by Mr Capon speaking for the tenants, who also referred to the previous owner, Joseph Shuttleworth, Frank's father, as the benefactor of the estate as well as to the memory of the Rev Robert Lang and how appreciative they all were to have the descendants of both, particularly Dorothy as the 'light and sunshine of the village` in their midst. Mr Lee endorsed all that had been said then thanked the agent, Mr Munckton, for all he did. At that moment Mr Munckton had just left the marquee to supervise the next part of the festivities but, upon returning, said that, having been agent for 21 years, he hoped to continue for the next 21 years. In his speech, he referred to his recommendations of earlier years to lower the rents during a time of agricultural hardship, which had enabled the farming tenants to remain on their farms and he confirmed that his employer was always ready to hear any suggestions as to what would assist his tenants.

Despite the terrible weather that day, there were sports events both for the grownups and for the children, amongst which were flat races, hurdles and high jumps, egg and spoon races, a wheelbarrow race, an obstacle race and hilarious donkey races where one donkey refused to budge and another wouldn't accept a rider; there were bicycles dressed up for a competition in which the ladies participated. The vicar started the races, Dorothy's brothers were the sports stewards and their wives the judges for the cycle parades.

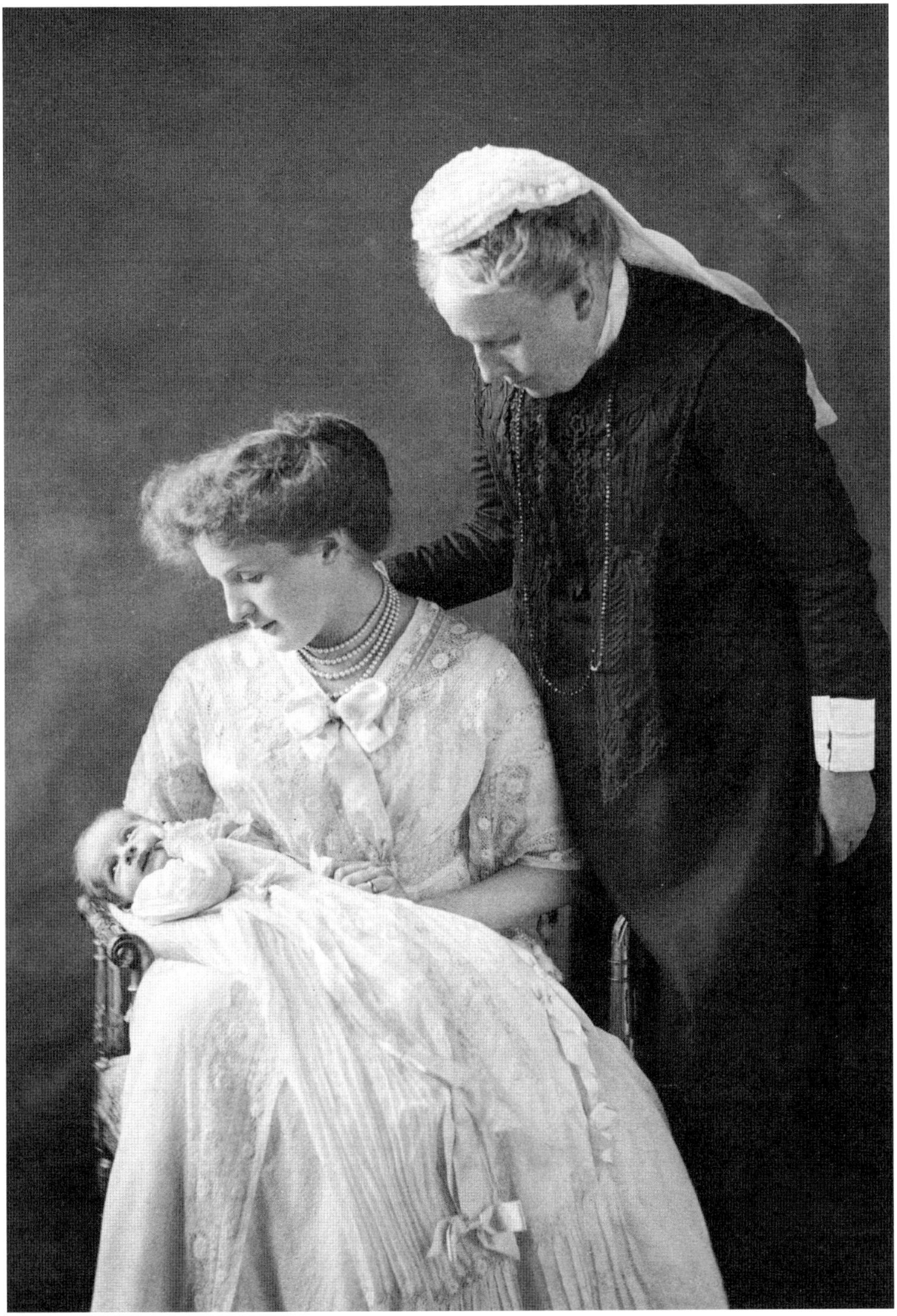

Adine Lang with Dorothy Clotilda Shuttleworth and grandson
Richard Ormonde Shuttleworth c.1909

The first years of Richard's life are well documented photographically. A Baby Book produced by the court photographer, Speaight Ltd, starts with a formal photograph of Frank and Dorothy with the baby wearing his christening robes, followed by another with his grandmother, Adine, in widow's dress looking down at her new grandchild held by his mother, then one photograph of the two nurses in attendance, Nurse Joyce and Nurse Fletcher. In September of the same year the family is visiting Alfred Shuttleworth at his Red Court home in Scarborough, which became a tradition for every summer from then on during Alfred's life.

When Richard was six months old his much beloved nanny, Susannah Wenham, arrived and stayed for nine years until she left to be married. With her loving care and example, she had a wonderful influence on him according to his mother. When she died unexpectedly, Richard was 17 and with a tutor in France and he wrote to his mother saying how much he had loved her and that there was not a better woman on this earth.

Nurse Wenham with Richard Ormonde Shuttleworth 1909

Frank Shuttleworth with two year old Richard Ormonde Shuttleworth

There are many photos showing Richard as a small child - on a donkey in Scarborough aged just a year beside his father mounted on 'Blue Ribbon' and then the first photos of him on a small pony called 'Bo Peep' which were taken when he was about three and half, the year before his father was to die. Visits to Cowes and photos taken with his father on the yacht document the summer when he was two, and others show him barefoot with a spade on the beach at Deauville together with Dr Lawrence who was attending Frank, whose heart ailments continued to be a worry. The following year, there are photographs taken on the beach at Salcombe and the next summer at Scarborough with other small children. A professional photograph taken that year (1912) is as if the three-year-old was addressing a meeting. This was framed and fondly entitled 'The Labour Speaker'.

The annual Old Warden village school treat was celebrated every year and planned to take place on or about Richard's birthday in mid-July, with a tea party with sports for young and old whilst the Band of the Bedfordshire Yeomanry played and each child received a present from Dorothy.

Richard Ormonde Shuttleworth aged three, known as the 'speaker in Hyde Park'

Children at the beach in Scarborough with their nannies c.1913

Richard Ormonde Shuttleworth shrimping at Scarborough 1913/14

1912 Wolsey

The first motor cars were invented during the last years of the nineteenth century but it was not until 1912 that Frank decided to buy a car and ordered a Wolsey Model M5. It was a four/six seat limousine with a 23 hp engine and maximum speed of 50mph. A few weeks before Frank died, the local press reported that Dorothy had been driving in Luton and had a collision with a cart which was somewhat damaged but that she was unhurt so she had already learnt to drive. For many years, this car was used to take guests and their luggage to the railway station in Biggleswade and the car is still in the Shuttleworth Collection today.

The first flight in an aeroplane built by the Wright Brothers in America was successful in 1903 after Lilienthal had been killed in Germany during his own experiments whilst producing a flying machine. The Wright brothers based their aeroplane on gliders and spent many years perfecting the design so, when Richard was born in 1909, cars and aeroplanes were beginning to dominate the inventions made in various countries. The Bleriot aeroplane he was later to take over from Albert Grimmer and fully repair, was the twin of the first plane to fly across the British Channel the same year as Richard was born.

It was in May of 1910 that King Edward VII had died and was succeeded by his son, George V who was married to Mary of Teck.

Dorothy with three year old Richard by Frank Dicksee 1913

Frank Shuttleworth's death

On Jan 31st 1913, Frank died unexpectedly in his 68th year at the Shuttleworths' London house in Berkeley Square. He had been in touch with his doctor a few days before and had driven to London to be near him but died after a heart attack that night, before Dr Lawrence could be there. Dorothy was by his bedside until the end. The previous years there were repeatedly signs that he had not been very well and there is a photograph of Dorothy pulling him in a small cart while he carries one of the surviving chins and it is believed he would also have been attended by the setters, Bruin and Balfour, but they don't appear in the picture.

The funeral took place at Old Warden and Frank was buried in the family vault in the graveyard of St Leonard's Church. The coffin, laid on a farm wagon, was drawn by powerful farm horses as Frank had wished, from the House through the

Frank Shuttleworth in small cart with Dorothy Clotilda Shuttleworth pulling Jan 1913

park and village up to the church. It was covered with a Union Jack upon which was placed his regimental plumed helmet and sword and the wreaths from his wife, small son and brother. Following behind the coffin, was his favourite horse led by the head groom, Foster, carrying the reversed military boots and wearing the pall of the 7th Hussars.

The service was held by two of Dorothy's brothers and an uncle who were all clergymen, assisted by the vicar of Southill. Mr Birch again played the organ, the hymns and psalms being chosen by the family and, at the grave the choir sang the Nunc Dimitis. Three volleys were then fired and a trumpet sounded the Last Post. The weather was very bad - cold and wet, increasingly so as the day went on. As the church was very full with guests, the local parishioners were asked to allow the guests coming from afar to be seated inside the church, whilst they crowded in at the back. All the employees from the whole estate as well as all the servants from the house and tenants and neighbours attended the funeral as did the wide circle of friends. Over one hundred wreaths were laid on the vault where Frank was buried beside his father, Joseph, who had died thirty years before. At the same time, a memorial service was held at St Swithin's church in Lincoln, attended by all the local dignitaries and the managers and employees of the Clayton and Shuttleworth factory at Stamp End. The church at Biggleswade held a special service recognising all Frank had done over many years for that town.

Frank had left a will whereby Trustees were appointed to run the estate. These were his brother, Alfred Shuttleworth, the lawyer W.F Fletcher from Biggleswade, and Nathaniel Cockburn who was linked to the family, his mother being a Clayton. The agent, Mr Tom Munckton who had been at Old Warden since 1888, knew the estate extremely well and also knowing all the tenants and employees very well, thereby assured the continuation of the management of the Shuttleworth estate. He had originally been in the Yeomanry when Frank raised the regiment and, in due course, Munckton was a member of the County Council so, with his wide local experience, he was well able to assist the smooth transition to the new situation, and he was to continue as agent until 1930. The local solicitor, Mr Fletcher from Biggleswade, looked after the legal side and Alfred was to help Dorothy who, as the years went by, involved herself more and more in the estate and the needs of the village. She also had some help from her elder brother, Robert Charles Vaughan Lang who, when one of the original ones died, became a Trustee, as did Dorothy herself. The shooting Frank had built up during so many years was to continue organised by Lord Westmorland who had been a good friend and a famous shot.

Dorothy Clotilda Shuttleworth as a widow with Richard Ormonde Shuttleworth 1913

Childhood photographs of Richard with his mother dressed in black take up some pages in this childhood album and other children appear too on the photographs. They were cousins and visiting friends seen in the gardens at Old Warden and there are photographs of a group of small children shrimping, presumably in Scarborough, taken in the summer following the death of Frank. Dorothy's nephew, Vaughan Lang, who was just a few years older than Richard, used to spend part of the summer holidays at the sea-side with them and also appears in the photographs.

Visiting children in the garden at Old Warden Park c.1913

Chapter 9

Dorothy remarries, and the First World War

Barely a year and a half after the death of Frank Shuttleworth and just before the First World War broke out, Dorothy married again to William McClaren Campbell who had been a friend of Frank's for many years and was also quite some years older than Dorothy, having been born in Glasgow in 1864. He was an exceedingly good looking and charming man, known amongst his contemporaries as 'William the Conqueror.' He was the son of the second marriage of Archibald Campbell VI of Glendaruel who died when William was only ten, and Christina McClaren. His eldest half-brother died aged 21 in Tobago and his half-sisters were married when he was still a small child. He had two sisters, Anne Louisa and Alice Mary, to whom he was very close and he used to return to Glendaruel as a young soldier as often as he had the chance to do so although the property was sold before the turn of the century by his elder half-brother's heir. His mother, Christina McClaren, was the daughter of a wealthy merchant from Glasgow, William McClaren and his wife, Mary Butterworth Runcorn, and was one of eight siblings, The McClarens had a thriving manufacturing and trading company with a branch in Manchester and, in the mid nineteenth century when William's parents married, they were living in a large house on Woodland Terrace near Kelvingrove Park, just outside Glasgow.

From 1877-1881 William went to Wellington College in Berkshire, a school much frequented by army families, then to university in St Andrews from where he went on to Sandhurst. At an early age, he joined the 42nd Regiment (Black Watch), a regiment in which every ancestor of his had served back to the raising of the regiment in the 18th century. The Campbells of Glendaruel were descended from the then Earls of Argyll in the 17th century via Campbell of Lochnell and Campbell

William McClaren Campbell sitting on stone bannister c.1914

of Jura. They were very intermarried and their property had passed various times through the female line. William was often a guest at Inverary of his kinsman, the Duke of Argyll, who was married to Princess Louise, a daughter of Queen Victoria.

William Campbell and Dorothy had links if not a relationship in that Sir Colin Campbell, who lifted the siege of Lucknow during the Indian Mutiny, was the son of a Campbell aunt, a sister of William's grandfather, which would explain why the entrance to the manse at Glendaruel was built as a copy of the Gates of Lucknow. They still stand to this day despite the house itself having burnt down. Dorothy's uncle, Col Arthur Moffat Lang, who was a Chief Engineer was, together with General Sir Colin Campbell, instrumental in lifting the siege of Lucknow and was assured by him that he would receive a VC for his bravery. Arthur Lang was mentioned three times for a VC but never received it as it was said all he did was in the course of his duty. Lang had then joined General Sir Hope-Grant's column in Oudh - yet another uncle who was married to a sister of Dorothy's mother.

William had been stationed in various parts of the British Empire during his military career, serving in Gibraltar and in Burma as ADC to the General Richard Campbell Stewart, a second cousin. He was then military secretary to the Governor of Madras. He fought in the Boer War and was one of the adjutants to the Viceroy, Lord Curzon, in India during the famous Durbar of 1903. He was made an MVO in 1906 and, at the next Durbar in India in 1911, he was given a medal by George V. He was still in Calcutta in the spring of 1914 when he was Adjutant to the Governor General but, in the summer of that year, he returned to England when he and Dorothy married.

As mentioned, William was a friend of Frank Shuttleworth's and appears in the visitors' books both at shoots at Old Warden as well as being a guest on the yacht in Cowes Week and on board during a Scottish cruise. There is also a charming photograph of the two men wearing jaunty hats with two ladies riding bicycles taken at an earlier date. William and Dorothy's wedding took place in London at St Columba's, the Scottish Church in Pont Street, barely a week before the First World War was declared and then William, who had the rank of Colonel, was appointed to command the 2nd battalion of the Black Watch so, as war broke out, William had to leave to join his regiment which was arriving back from India, landing at Marseille and then progressing to Lille in the North of France where they took up their positions preparing for the coming trench warfare.

Frank Shuttleworth, Lady Clemy Waring, William McClaren Campbell, unknown c.1890

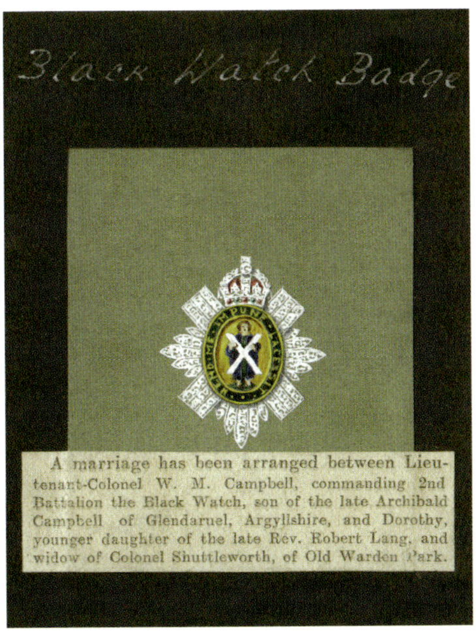

A marriage has been arranged between Lieutenant-Colonel W. M. Campbell, commanding 2nd Battalion the Black Watch, son of the late Archibald Campbell of Glendaruel, Argyllshire, and Dorothy, younger daughter of the late Rev. Robert Lang, and widow of Colonel Shuttleworth, of Old Warden Park.

Dorothy Clotilda Shuttleworth & William McClaren Campbell marriage announcement
and Black Watch brooch design

World War I

The murder of The Austrian Crown Prince and his wife in Sarajevo resulted in an Austrian ultimatum to the Serbs who were thought to have engineered the murder. The German Emperor supported Austria and the Russians supported Serbia. The Germans invaded Belgium and the English and French were bound by a treaty to come to its aid so the terrible First World War erupted after a peace in Europe which had lasted about forty years. The continent was now to be engulfed by a conflict which decimated the then living generation of young men throughout Europe, robbing the future generation of possible new and strong leaders.

Straight after the beginning of hostilities, the trench warfare in northern France dominated the fighting which historians still argue about, blaming the generals in charge for sending wave after wave of young soldiers to attack the enemy when the advances were limited to a few yards at a time, in which both sides were 'bogged' down. This was a traumatic experience for the troops, stuck as they were in the muddy trenches for month after month which was extremely debilitating with endemic disease rampant. It was also emotionally shattering, especially for those in a responsible position having to obey higher orders yet probably also doubting the plans of the military leadership directing the operations.

William, who was a very sensitive and intellectually interested character with a strong sense of responsibility, suffered a total breakdown of his health with what then came to be called 'shell-shock' and he had to be hospitalised during that first winter of the war. This was coupled with further physical illnesses, possibly pneumonia and Trench or enteric fever which spread via the rat-infested trenches which, during the wet winter weather, were debilitating and horrific with rats crawling over the refuse and the numerous dead and wounded having to be carried to the first aid posts behind the lines.

Today we would say William suffered from emotional trauma. Dorothy, like the majority of people at that time, did not know what 'shell-shock' entailed and feared that William had developed a mental disease which also caused her much worry and stress.

As soon as it became possible, he was sent to an auxiliary hospital near North Berwick in Scotland on the south shore of the Firth of Forth, before going to Ireland the following summer to recover, looked after by his younger sister, Alice, whose husband Ralph Carr-Ellison was Lieut. Col and Assistant Quartermaster General, Irish Command stationed in Dublin at the time.

Brig. Gen. William McClaren Campbell in Black Watch Uniform c.1914

Dorothy was already nursing with the Red Cross in Bedford when William was invalided out and she was about to open Old Warden as a convalescent home, having welcomed Belgian refugees immediately after the declaration of war. She had first offered her newly-built house in Upper Grosvenor Street, London as a hospital, which was used for officers for a short while and then Old Warden Park opened as a Red Cross Convalescent Home providing 15 beds in the spring of 1915 and continued until the following spring taking in soldiers for convalescence who had been first at Kempston Military Hospital at Bedford where Dorothy was nursing twice a week. During those months, 90 patients passed through the convalescent home, all paid for by the estate as no government grant was given. The government was only interested in continuing to use Old Warden if at least 40 beds could be supplied. Dorothy was the Commandant under the Bedfordshire Branch of the Red Cross whose chairman was Lady Ampthill. During those war years, the estate also paid for the salary, board and lodging of a cook and also a masseur. Dorothy was still nursing at Kempston during the last year of the war, even after the birth of her daughter, Anne Elspeth Campbell, born in August 1917 as her personnel card issued for Jan to Dec 1918 shows.

William McClaren Campbell with Dorothy and their daughter Anne, born in August 1917

Due to her local obligations, she was unable to nurse William herself or help his recovery but, taking Richard with her, she did spend some months at North Berwick in the summer of 1915, presumably close to where William had been hospitalised. Dorothy needed rest herself, having been through much emotional stress as well as physical with the running of the convalescent homes and nursing in Bedford, apart from the worry about her husband of just a few months. North Berwick was at that time a very fashionable seaside resort and she and the six-

The Governess Miss Hayward with deck chair on the beach, North Berwick 1915

Richard Ormonde Shuttleworth with cousin Vaughan Lang on beach c.1915

year-old Richard stayed at the Marine Hotel during July and August of 1915. Mrs Waby, the Housekeeper, seems to have been there too and Tom Munckton, the agent, reported news from Old Warden and was sent a postcard by Richard. There are photographs taken on a beach that year either at North Berwick or perhaps on the annual visit to Scarborough. Richard is shown with his cousin, Vaughan Lang. who was a few years older and Miss Hayward, the governess, is also present.

At the beginning of the war, a large number of Belgian refugees arrived in Britain and some were given lodgings in Bedfordshire. Dorothy volunteered to take in some of the refugees, amongst which the family of Col Jardine were given rooms at the House at Old Warden, another family was in the village, further refugee families were staying at Broom, in some of the Whitbreads' cottages and a family of four was staying in a house on the Whitbread estate. In January 1915, a Bedfordshire Belgian Refugees' Day was held in the Bedford Town Hall. Presents for the children were collected throughout the county and many inhabitants gave donations and money towards their upkeep. A Belgian professor gave a talk on the position of the refugees in relation to their hosts then a concert took place and tea was served before the presents were distributed, after which competitions were held followed by dancing before ending at 8pm with the playing of the National Anthem. A Belgian official Committee was set up in 1914 to give advice to Belgian refugees but it seems that most of the refugees came partly on invitation of their hosts or by recommendation and, when a committee was set up in Bedford with members of the local County Council, it was also found that most of the refugees had come by private invitation. The agent, Mr Munckton, reported to Shire Hall in Bedford that help was mainly coming from private sources. Dorothy had equipped a five-room cottage in the village with new furniture and was providing everything required, as well as looking after the family staying in the House. How long the Belgians stayed, I have not been able to establish, but I presume they could not return to Belgium until all hostilities had ceased

Sometime later as William's health improved after the months of recuperation in Ireland, he was posted to the Reserves Command in Derbyshire and he was assisting in organising the Old Warden shoots during those winters as there is correspondence between him and the agent, Munckton, about details concerning the shoots, albeit Lord Westmorland having been appointed by Frank's will to run the shooting until Richard should come of age. On Boxing Day in 1915, despite the war, the local newspaper reported that a large shooting party was held in the woods around Northill and there are photographs showing some of the shots

Dorothy with daughter Anne by Speaight c.1922

wearing army uniform. It seems that William Campbell had recovered enough to be present. He had just been appointed Brigadier General to the reserves in Derby after the months of recuperation in Ireland. During 1916, he was first stationed at Richmond in Yorkshire, moving then to Farnborough before spending quite some months in Aldershot and then Colchester.

Dorothy visited him at some of his military bases, otherwise they met in London where their baby daughter Anne, my mother, was born in August 1917 in the Upper Grosvenor Street house. The attending gynaecologist was Dr Gilliat who a generation later attended my birth in December 1938, making me the first grandchild he delivered. There is only one known photograph of Anne as a baby with both parents, William being in uniform as he was then still stationed in Colchester and then an official one of Dorothy with the new baby and her eight-year-old son, Richard.

William received a CBE in 1919 before retiring in the summer of that year. After the war ended, he helped to raise funds to establish the Black Watch Memorial Home at Dunalastair in Dundee, of which he became the first chairman and, upon retiring - again due to continuing ill health, he remained the chairman of the Executive Committee. In 1920, he was living in Dundee and was sending out letters applying for financial contributions to aid the home. It seems that William had hoped that Dorothy would move to live with him in Scotland where he was then still stationed after the end of the war. She was though tied to Old Warden by the conditions of the Trust which had been set up for the duration of the minority of Richard and she could not move away or take Richard with her without forfeiting her financial assets or leaving Richard alone at Old Warden. The circumstances of those years did not enable William and Dorothy to ever live the regular life of a married couple together. Each had their responsibilities to fulfil and the situation was not in their favour. Anne, aged about four, did then spend some time with her father in Scotland before his health further deteriorated.

William's untimely and unexpected death aged 60 in June 1924 was whilst on a trip to Brussels. He was possibly there to visit the grave of his grandfather, Neil Campbell, who had been killed at the Battle of Waterloo in 1815 and to see a memorial that had been erected in an old church close to the battlefield where the names of all the officers and men of the 79th Regiment were engraved on a white marble monument about which he had been corresponding some years previously. That year – 1924 - on Waterloo Day the Times reproduced the newspaper of the day of the battle on 18th June 1815, the centennial not having been commemorated in 1915, as the First World War was then raging.

William had appointed his nephew, Jock Carr-Ellison as guardian to his daughter Anne and he then had to travel out to Brussels to bring back the coffin after William's sudden death and accompany it to Glendaruel where he was buried in the family graveyard. Glendaruel, which lies to the south of Loch Fyne and opens out into the Kyles of Bute, was where William had grown up. As mentioned earlier, the property had been sold some years prior to the end of the nineteenth century, but the graveyard continued to be used by the family of the Campbells of Glendaruel. It is a hauntingly beautiful spot on the crest of a small hill, the cemetery set amongst large beech trees and surrounded by a now rather crumbling wall, with sheep wandering in and out. The last Campbell relation was buried there in the 1980s.

Dorothy attended the funeral at Glendaruel which, according to press reports, was a very impressive and emotional ceremony with the Black Watch pipers playing the dirge as the coffin was borne from the church. Various relations were present and members of the Black Watch Depot at Perth were in attendance, as was his successor commanding the 2nd Battalion, Col Sutherland, accompanied by pipers and buglers. Many of the mourners wore a sprig of bog-myrtle, the Clan Campbell emblem. The coffin was born by NCOs to the burial ground on the hill while pipers played the 'Flowers of the Forest' and 'Lochaber no More' and a Black Watch bugler sounded the Last Post. There were numerous floral tributes including a wreath from the Dunalastair Home of which William was the first president.

The Glendaruel estate had been sold by William's nephew who had emigrated to New Zealand. The new owners then tore down the old house and built a stone manse on the site but this house burnt down in the later years of the 1960s and the site is now run as a caravan park. Only the Gates of Lucknow are still standing as a memorial to the family. As mentioned above, these gates had been built in recognition of General Sir Colin Campbell's successful lifting of the siege of Lucknow during the Indian Mutiny; his mother had been a sister of the then Campbell of Glendaruel, and William's father, Archibald Campbell VI of Glendaruel, also served in the 42nd Highland Regiment which too, had been active at Lucknow.

Chapter 10

Dorothy and her children at Old Warden

Towards the end of the war in September 1918, a Red Cross fete was held at Old Warden Park to raise money for the Kempston hospital where Dorothy was still nursing part time. The fete was opened by Lady Halsey representing Lady Ampthill, the President of the Bedfordshire Red Cross. Lady Halsey was the wife of Admiral Sir Lionel Halsey, a leading commander in the Royal Navy in command of the 2nd Battlecruiser Squadron of the Grand Fleet, present at the German surrender at Scapa Flow and very much instrumental in forwarding the Allies' naval advance in the war. The Halseys had just moved to Old Warden to live at Mount Pleasant, a house on the estate. At the fete, there were numerous stalls and an exhibition of wonderful work made by blinded soldiers. Picture frames, mats and baskets were offered for sale, as well as county produce and the usual popular lucky dip and bran tub.

After the war in October 1920, there was a Women's Institute Fair held at Old Warden Park presided over by Dorothy with an exhibition of lace made by the Belgian refugees. She had been given a tablecloth with lace insets showing the Shuttleworth coat of arms and another centre piece where the arms of the Allies were worked in circles of about a yard in diameter, another identical one had been presented to the Queen of the Belgians.

In the years after the end of the First World War and during the following decades after Dorothy had been widowed a second time, she continued her life based at Old Warden but with short weekly visits to London, a routine which continued until she reached a very old age. Whilst Dorothy's children were young, she would have other children to come and play, some of them were Dorothy's

Anne Elspeth Campbell with dolls c.1922

brothers' children who would come to stay or accompany them to the seaside but also children of friends of hers sometimes came too. As mentioned previously, when she took the children to the seaside, there are photographs of Richard shrimping with friends' children and there are other photographs with children taken in the garden at Old Warden or down at the lake sailing one of the model boats. Recently I spoke to a now very elderly lady who had been sent as a small child to stay at Old Warden whilst her parents were away and she confirmed to me how kind Dorothy had been to her but that she had been rather awed and even scared of Richard, then nearly grown up and of my mother, Anne, a young teenager. I presume that, as most of the time they were usually the only children in the house, they were neither of them very used to any children of different ages staying and, being quite far from the village, they did not have many local children they would regularly meet to play with.

Although Trustees had been appointed to run the estate together with the agent, all through the childhood of her children Dorothy was involved in the day to day management, sitting at her desk in the study as from 9am and receiving the heads of all departments, whether it be the household, the gardens or even the farm. I remember her telling me that she had been taught by her father to stand up to receive anyone coming into the room and she continued that throughout her life. She was a very disciplined and charming personality with a strong sense of responsibility, not only towards her close family but to all living on the estate or in the village in which she was so very much involved, and had been since her teenage years, looking after anyone ill and caring for the mothers of new babies to whom she always presented a bassinet at birth.

Dorothy continued the annual Old Warden Cottage Garden Competition which Frank Shuttleworth had instituted in 1903 and which was meant to encourage the tenants to grow fruit and vegetables as well as flowers. She became the president of the local Women's Institute and, in 1920 she had a suitable hut built in the village for their meetings and activities and, the following year at the second Exhibition of the Bedford County Federation, she was one of the dignitaries and organised a stall of interesting exhibits: a pencil used to sign the Peace of Versailles in 1919 by the German delegate, Müller, a Maori cloak from New Zealand lent by Admiral Sir Lionel Halsey, some Honiton lace and further embroidery. In 1929, at the annual Home crafts Exhibition and sale, Dorothy herself won first prize for quilting and the Old Warden Women's Institute won the first prize overall.

Other organisations Dorothy was actively helping were the Biggleswade Workhouse where most years the inmates were invited to visit the gardens at Old Warden Park and were given tea afterwards; she organised fetes in the gardens in aid of the Primrose League and twice she invited about 150 ex-servicemen to dinner at Old Warden with evening entertainment. One year Richard had to read out a telegram with best wishes from the Admiral then accompanying the Prince of Wales on his World Tour. She opened the Park and the Gardens regularly for many different organisations, even the Biggleswade Farmers and Butchers would be invited to hold their annual holiday outing at Old Warden Park. Dorothy was also made vice president of the Cricket Club, when her son, aged 12, became the president.

Dorothy's work with the Red Cross continued from the war years on and, as from September 1922, she was Vice President of the Biggleswade Red Cross and Commandant of the Bedfordshire VAD Detachment (Women's Voluntary Aid Detachment) organising a collection during the Red Cross Week. Dorothy was involved in the setting up of a Medical Supply Depot for Biggleswade in a building supplied by the solicitor, W. Fletcher, who was also one of the Trustees for the Shuttleworths. Sick room appliances and stores could be hired by anyone presenting a doctor's order. This continued with Dorothy as Commandant until 1930 when a new basis was sought to continue the work as Dorothy felt she could no longer financially maintain the Clinic and a way was found to assure the continuation under the Biggleswade Urban Council and a new Committee of Management was set up.

Dorothy was elected President of the Biggleswade Women's Conservative Unionist Association in 1923 and re-elected in 1927 and she was known to encourage all those she could to vote for the Conservative party.

The church continued to play a large role in her life, perhaps one of her few weaknesses was that, as patron of the living, she did not always have a happy hand in choosing a new vicar and so, over the years, there were many changes of incumbents.

Richard was taught at an early age to prepare himself to take over responsibility for the estate and to start by making a small welcoming speech or reading an address at any of the village functions or when entertaining the tenants. In 1920, the Prince of Wales came over from Sandringham to visit the Halseys with their two little daughters at Mount Pleasant and Dorothy and the teenage Richard were presented, after which the Prince then shook hands and chatted with two ex-servicemen before continuing his drive to London.

During Richard's early childhood, attempts had been made to give him music lessons and he started off trying to learn to play the violin, having lessons with Miss Helen Willett who came from Bedford. In due course, she came to be employed as secretary/companion to Dorothy and moved to Old Warden where she became invaluable in all aspects of Dorothy's activities and lived there for the rest of her life

In the meantime, Anne who was still a small child, was alone in the nursery at Old Warden during term times, whilst her brother was away at boarding school. She had a much-loved Swiss nurse-maid called Pierette to teach her French which apparently she spoke before English. Aged about four or somewhat older, she went under the care of her nurse-maid to visit her father in Perth where he was building up the Black Watch Memorial Home at Dunalastair in nearby Dundee but her memories of the visit were limited to complaining that her feet grew so fast and her father would not buy her new shoes. Anne was only seven when her father sadly died unexpectedly in Brussels and she always regretted having seen so little of him. Her cousin, Jock Carr-Ellison, his mother having been a sister of William, was named her guardian. She continued to live with her mother and half-brother at Old Warden but accounts for her upbringing were sent to her guardian, who managed her father's inheritance on her behalf until she came of age.

Aware as Dorothy was of carrying the responsibility for the Shuttleworth inheritance, she decided it would be more suitable to take back the name of Shuttleworth. After William died in 1924, she applied for a name change by deed poll which was announced in the London Gazette on 3rd September 1926; a logical decision but one which was always to rankle with my mother (her daughter) who felt that she, being called Anne Campbell, was seen to be just a foundling or even a second-class citizen at Old Warden, which I am sure Dorothy did not intend and surely she tried to reassure her small daughter on all points.

Richard turned eight in 1917, the summer his sister was born and, being already of learning age, he had a governess called Miss Hayward who came to teach him, remaining a much-valued family friend until her death in 1938. Once when he was grown up, she bravely let him take her up in one of his early planes, the Moth, and he even took her as a passenger on his motorbike. There is a photograph showing the resilient elderly lady striding along the beach with a deckchair under her arm.

A Miss Gough then came to prepare him for school. In the summer of 1918, he went first to a prep school, which had its school buildings at St Peters Court at Broadstairs, but had been evacuated to Tisbury when the war started and then, after only one term, he was moved to St Aubyns at Rottingdean, a prep school run by his uncle, Robert Charles Vaughan Lang, his mother's unmarried eldest brother. His letters home from there were mainly full of questions as to how everyone was getting on in Old Warden, but he was proud of his little sister who, in 1921 aged 4, won the sisters' race at the school summer open day.

He was there until, in 1922 aged 13, he passed, with the help of a special tutor (crammer) into Eton to the house of a Mr Catley. His school life was never a great success. He was not good at passing exams and the ordinary school subjects did not really gain his interest, which was purely concentrated on mechanics and related experiments. Aged 16, after only three years at Eton, he was superannuated for having attempted an experiment with explosives which blew a hole in the bath.

Maybe today he would have been found to be dyslexic, a condition inherited by his great nephews and nieces. I would have thought that it would have been far better to have sent him to a technical college rather than trying to give him the typical upper-class education of the period.

Why Eton was chosen when his mother's family were all old Harrovians is also a riddle to me, especially when taking into consideration how his father had been given a very international education. Maybe this inspired Dorothy to decide that, after leaving Eton, he was to be sent off with a tutor to stay with a family in Versailles, where he went to the Lycée Hoche there. With crammer lessons by a further tutor, he passed as 2nd out of 80 in chemistry and science. He then went to Tours with a Mr Hursley staying in a local pension, where he learnt perfect French.

Dorothy drove out to see him on various occasions taking him to visit the chateaux on the Loire, the gothic cathedrals (all photographed by her father in his youth) and other historical sites. Once she decided to teach her children the 'simple' way of travelling by buying a caravan and, accompanied by the chauffeur and a lady's maid, attempted to camp in France. Her rather one-sided attempts at cooking ended in a fire and so back to the comfort of a hotel.

The Dolls House

When Anne was eight years old, her brother Richard broke his leg and, to occupy him and keep him quiet, Dorothy and he decided to build a dolls house for Anne. They used two polished walnut linen cupboards and divided them up to create 22 rooms. Dorothy and Richard laid the parquet floors and panelled the rooms as well as installing the stairs in both cabinets and Richard also laid the necessary electric wires to illuminate the rooms. The left cabinet had the grander rooms: drawing room, hall and dining room on the ground floor and, on the first floor, the main bedroom, dressing room and a bathroom and above were the nursery and night nursery. The second cabinet had the kitchen and the pantry on the ground floor with the housekeeper's room beside it. Above on the first floor were a library and the boudoir or ladies' sitting room and, on the top floor were the school room and some bedrooms.

The dolls were made by Dorothy and were meant to represent the real family and the servants at Old Warden: Mrs Cave, the cook- housekeeper, Everett, the

The Dolls House

The Dolls House detail

Butler and a footman called Jack, a few kitchen maids and a parlour maid as well as the family living there: mother, grandfather and grandmother, some children and a nanny as well as a governess. Dorothy made the curtains and framed some photographs of paintings in the house as well as some Chinese rice-paper paintings of costumed figures to hang on the walls. Some of the bedrooms were papered with patterned wallpaper and carpets were cut from embroidery or pieces of velvet. Most of the furniture was made at Westacre in East Anglia where a charity organisation was founded by a lady called Ysabel Birkbeck who occupied refugee children with making these charming little models of English furniture, as well as lacquer pieces, and four poster beds all with handmade linen and covers. These were offered for sale at specially chosen shops in London and the proceeds were given to charity after the children had been paid a few shillings for their work and involvement. The kitchen and pantry were full of miniature pots and pans and the china dining and tea sets, apparently from Limoges, which were said to be reject items from those made for the 'Queen's Dolls House' built for Queen Mary by the famous architect, Lutyens, a few years previously. The dining room had small silver models of candlesticks, coffee jugs, and tea pots etc which were of Dutch origin.

The Dolls House detail

Towards the end of World War II, when I was a small child of about five living for nearly half a year with my grandmother, I had the greatest delight in unpacking and setting up the dolls house again, assisted by my grandmother. It had been packed away and stored with other furnishings in the Boudoir whilst the house was once again a convalescent home. Now the dolls house is on view at the Castle of Langenburg in the south of Germany which is the home of my son and his family but it is open to the public and may be visited.

The highlights of Anne's childhood years were when Richard came home from boarding school bringing friends with him. In 1927, he was at a crammer's in Lathbury near Newport Pagnell, where his greatest and enduring friend was Archie Edmunds or 'Jimmy', as he was known to some friends. He remained Richard's life-long closest friend and, much later, he wrote a very endearing and entertaining memory about Richard and all the escapades they had together. Firstly, reminiscences from Lathbury where he was allowed to keep a pony and even ride with the local hunt, then on to Sandhurst, then the beginning of his racing career and the first aeroplanes he bought himself, up to his death in 1940.

The head of the school at Lathbury was a Mr Trevor who summed up Richard's abilities - and weaknesses - to a tee, assessing his character and reassuring his mother that, although he was very young for his age, he was physically as hard as nails, always meaning to do his best, and, when ticked off for playing the fool, was full of remorse promising to try harder next time. Richard was confirmed when he was 17 by the Bishop of Barking after having been instructed by a Mr Hinde, rector of Islington who described him as 'a true Nathaniel without guile'.

Richard needed to take his school certificate to pass into the army, so he went to Oxford with some other pupils to sit the exams but fell asleep during one of them, having been given an eggnog to boost him, and so failed that one but he did succeed in getting two credits: one for scripture taught him by his mother and one for French!

It had been decided that, when he was 18 he was not to go into the Hussars where his father had been for many years but into the 16th Lancers where Colonel Diggle had served. Colonel Diggle was not yet the estate agent at that time, still just a friend of the family. Richard was stationed at Tidworth when he joined in 1927. He had his mare 'Spearlass' and his Alsatian 'Woolfie' with him and had polo lessons at Hurlingham. Then he also learnt to fly and bought himself a small plane, a Moth, keeping this a secret from his mother, although she apparently did suspect it. This seems to be the beginning of his escapades in racing and flying.

The Pageant

In the summer of 1926, Dorothy decided to have a pageant performed in the Swiss Garden. It was taken from the 'Masque of Life' written by Louis N. Parker. This Masque had originally been performed in July 1907 in the gardens of Claremont House in Surrey then lived in by the Duchess of Albany. At that time, it had been produced to raise money in aid of the Deptford Fund and was performed under the patronage of the King and Queen. Dorothy had taken part in the Third Vision dressed in a beautiful bright blue velvet gown as Anne Boleyn whilst Frank had acted as the Lord Chamberlain in the Fourth Vision.

Now Dorothy adapted the text of the Masque calling it the 'Origin of An English Name' with only three visions instead of the six in the original version.

The Masque portrayed the history of a typical English name in this case 'Smith'. There is a Questioner and Time who calls in Memory and together they present the story of the name, beginning with a procession of druids who are about

Pageant in the Swiss Garden 1926

to sacrifice a beautiful young girl who is rescued by her lover, a good looking young Briton who as a smith makes a cross out of the druid's sickle and so denotes the beginning of Christianity in England.

This scene is followed by the arrival of first a Roman, planting his standard in the earth saying 'Veni, Vidi, Vici!' followed then by a Dane and a Norman. The second Vision plays in the time of Henry I and a grandson of Smith is making a coat of mail, before fighting a duel for the right to marry the daughter of the Norman overlord. These scenes were acted down near the lake in a glade opening from the shrubbery with a winding path along which the characters appeared.

The Questioner and Memory now pass over a few centuries to portray how the clan of Smith fared in Tudor times. At this point, the spectators were asked to move to the Swiss Garden where the fourth vision unrolls on the lawn beneath the Swiss Cottage, whilst the audience sit on tiers of seats leading down from the cottage. Queen Elizabeth I is visiting Sir Walter Raleigh with her courtiers. Edmund Spenser reads from his masque, the Faerie Queene, and then Captain John Smith, having just returned from Virginia in America, so named in honour of the Queen, brings with him the beautiful native girl, Pocahontas, who had saved him from being killed by her Red Indian tribe. He then presents her to Queen Elizabeth. In the final scene, Memory is prevented from leaving by the Questioner and then Time reappears as a radiant youth.

The actors were all local residents, villagers, employees of the estate and house as well as Dorothy's sister in law, Amy Lang, who plays Queen Elizabeth, her daughter, Adeane Lang, who is the Questioner and Dorothy's own children, Richard aged 17, who is dressed first as a messenger and then as a page, and Anne aged 9, as a niece of the Queen. A silent film was made of the performance and the photograph taken at the time shows all the actors grouped together in front of the Swiss Cottage. The costumes were made locally except for the Tudor gown Queen Elizabeth wore which Dorothy had appeared in at the original masque in 1907. The masque was performed to raise money for the local Red Cross Depot and the Bedford County Hospital. Admission was one shilling and reserved seats half a crown each. Despite it being a charitable event, a customs and excise entertainment tax had to be levied on the 450 seats before the proceeds could be paid to the Red Cross. In the following years, Dorothy opened the gardens once a week during the summer months, charging one shilling a head, again to raise money for the Red Cross Depot.

The political situation in Europe in those years after the First World War was not favourable. The war was won by the Allies but the Russian Revolution in 1917 with the murder of the Tsar and his family had shattered Europe. The strict retributions demanded from Germany helped create an atmosphere in which fascism was able to develop, also partly encouraged by the heavy inflation which affected most countries culminating in the 1929 Stock Exchange crash in New York. In England, the General Strike called by the Trades Unions in 1926 almost paralysed the country. The miners were joined by the bus and rail drivers and the dock workers, as well as the iron and steel workers who went out on strike in sympathy, the aim being to force the government, under Prime Minister Baldwin, to prevent the miners' wages being reduced, combined with longer working hours. It is estimated that seven and a half million were on strike but many people throughout the country also volunteered to help keep the country running.

In 1920 the winning powers of the First World War created the League of Nations which was a forerunner of the United Nations but unfortunately without actual power or any strong influence. In the next decade, the Spanish Civil War erupted and Hitler, who had come to power in Germany in 1933, first forced the Allies to hand back the Saarland and then annexed part of the Czech Republic before walking into Austria in 1938, whilst in England, the abdication of Edward VIII nearly caused a constitutional crisis. In September 1938, a conference was held in Münich attended by Italy, France and England, the latter being represented by the Prime Minister, Neville Chamberlain who, upon returning, assured the population of 'peace in our time'.

There were also positive and exciting discoveries and developments: Lindberg made the first flight over the Atlantic in 1927 and, in 1932 Amelia Earhart did her solo flight to Australia. Winnie the Pooh had been published in 1926 and was immediately a much beloved story, the Tomb of Tutankhamun was discovered in 1922 and, in 1927, the BBC was founded - just to show the variety of achievements.

Chapter 11

Dorothy and the estate; Richard comes of age

When Dorothy married Frank in 1902, Tom Munckton had already been estate agent since 1888 and was involved in every detail of the running of the estate and of the house. He paid the servants, supervised the accounts and was relied upon for everything, reporting in person when the Shuttleworths were at home or by hand-written letters. After Frank died and Trustees were appointed, he carried even more responsibility helping Dorothy in every way and he was entrusted to carry on with all the management of the estate and to assist the smooth running of the house. He was a sound agriculturist and very popular with the tenants who regarded him as a personal friend, listening to their problems and worries and helping where he could. He enjoyed a good story, had great common sense and was also a very good shot and keen sportsman, helping to organise the shoots for the family up until his retirement. Mr Munckton had been born in Wimborne, Dorset and lived with his wife, Emily, and two children at Home Farm and then, upon retirement in 1930, having sadly lost his wife five years previously, he moved to Holly Lodge in Broom. He had been a member of the County Council representing the Northill District, serving on many committees and also of the Biggleswade Rural Council, as well as being a member of the Old Warden Parish Council. He had joined the Bedfordshire Yeomanry in 1900 where he was quartermaster serving under Colonel Shuttleworth when the regiment was raised.

In the summer of 1930 Tom Munckton finally retired after a record making 42 years of service as estate agent. At the reception marking the end of his employment, the solicitor of the estate, Mr W. Fletcher from Biggleswade, presented Mr Munckton with a silver salver on behalf of the Trustees of the Trust founded by Frank Shuttleworth to manage the property during Richard's minority. Just a few years later, in the spring of 1934, he died and the funeral was held at the Old Warden parish church attended by many who had known and worked with him for so many years. The Vicar, the Rev. McCarthy, paid him a great tribute saying how he would be remembered with much affection by many, having been a most gentle and kind-hearted personality respected for his help in many a way whenever needed. The funeral was attended by his daughter and son-in-law as well as by his former employer, Dorothy Shuttleworth, with her son, Richard, and numerous friends and neighbours from throughout the county.

Tom Munckton was succeeded by William Fellowes who had previously been agent to Major Gosling at his estate at Hassobury, living at Hazel End near Bishops Stortford. Fellowes was born in 1899 and educated at Winchester living at Cornbury where his father was agent to the Watneys, but the family home was Shotesham near Norwich, a house built by Soane at the beginning of the nineteenth century. Billy Fellowes had only been called up at the end of the First World War and was able to start his career as an agent soon after the war ended. When he took over as estate agent in Old Warden in 1930, he fast grew to be a much-valued friend of the family. He was a renowned good shot and fisherman but hunting was his favoured sport and also that of his wife, Jane Ferguson, whom he married in 1934 and they both hunted with the Fitzwilliam. Through Admiral Sir Lionel Halsey who had accompanied the Prince of Wales on his World tour, he was recommended to be appointed as the agent for the Royal estate of Sandringham. He agreed not to leave Old Warden before the summer of 1936 but his departure after only six years was much regretted. He had also been a member of the Rural District Council and, during his few years at Old Warden, he was renowned for a marvellous sense of humour and of the ridiculous. He was very helpful in many ways also to friends of the family for whom he would do small favours like ordering tyres for the car of a daughter of friends. According to his son, he wrote in his memoirs that the beauty of Dorothy had always impressed him enormously. My mother, Anne, had claimed that she was madly in love with him as a teenager.

The next estate agent to be appointed was Major, later Colonel, Wyndham Diggle who was a son of close friends of Frank, his mother, Lily Diggle, often being a guest on the yacht at Cowes Regatta Week and who helped Dorothy as a new bride to adapt to society life. His father, who had been in the navy, had so successfully invested in a coal mine in British Columbia that he was able to participate in Edwardian society and also became a member of the Royal Yacht Club. After the departure of Billy Fellowes, Col Diggle, known as 'Corky', moved to Old Warden to be the agent. His wife, Eve Crossland, was a niece of Lady Faringdon, and her father had been the agent at Buscot Park for the first Lord Faringdon. The Diggles had at first to move into the agent's house at Home Farm, but together with Richard, Dorothy was able to organise that the Diggles and their three sons who were still at boarding schools, should move into Orchard Grange, the larger late Georgian house in the village which had been the vicarage when Dorothy's father was vicar of Old Warden. The estate was able to exchange the vicarage with a smaller house, Beech Cottage in the village, next door to the Reading Room which remained the vicarage until recent times. An astonishing story is that the Diggles had to clear the attic of chicken droppings left by a much earlier vicar's prize winning white Dorking hens. The Diggles were already great friends of Dorothy's and became of enormous help to her in the village, the church and the Red Cross organisation. When the second World War broke out, Col Diggle was called up again, and, from memory I believe that James Robinson, who ran an estate agent's office in Bedford, took over managing the estate. He would come over at least once a week doing the rounds on a horse, possibly Dorothy's, as she had stopped riding once the war broke out. He would then come to tea in the house where a large tea cup was especially kept for him. He was known as 'Father' for some reason I am not aware of. After the war, by the early 1950s Edward Bennet had been employed as agent, again living in the agent's house at Home Farm.

Dorothy had hunted regularly with Frank who had been the master of the Cambridgeshire until he retired in 1903 but from then on, Dorothy seems to have been more involved with the Oakley Hunt. She was patron of the Hunt Balls on many occasions which were held in different locations from Bedford to larger country houses throughout the Hunt's area and she recounted to me as a child about how she had often led the jumps having had

Dorothy mounted for hunt with the Cambridgeshire c.1905

Richard Ormonde Shuttleworth in Lancers Uniform c.1931

a very reliable mount. Richard hunted as well, first at Lathbury when he was at the crammer's but continued to do so with the Oakley also when he was in the army training camp. In 1930 the Point to Point Ball was held at Old Warden, Richard having followed in his father's footsteps by winning point to point races riding his hunter Spearlass, upon which he also won the Subalterns Cup for his regiment in that same year.

In the early summer of 1931, Dorothy had a car crash in France. This accident prevented her hunting at the beginning of that season but she wanted to start again in February of the next year, 1932, when she considered buying another horse to replace the one that was somewhat too lively which she had bought from a Captain Farmer a few years before. She then required a quieter horse but which would still jump well. That year she had also presented the Hunt with a silver cup.

The car accident had happened near Fontainebleau when she was driving a Morris. She damaged her back and possibly also her neck as she had problems from then on turning around, especially whilst driving a car. The remains of the Morris were shipped back to England by the AA and sent to Oxford for the personal attention of Sir William Morris, being completely "smashed up" and "utterly destroyed". It had only been bought in January of that year.

In July of 1932, Richard finally reached the age of 23 which his father had decreed should be his coming of age and should be the end of the Trust. All the tenants and their wives from Old Warden, Broom, Cople, Goldington and Ickwell were invited to a lunch which 800 guests attended in a huge marquee set up beside the house. Tea was served after all the speeches and sport-entertainments amongst which there was a Punch and Judy show and, towards the end the day, there was a spectacular firework display.

Many neighbours, friends and relations were also present and there is a group portrait photograph which was taken showing them all gathered on the steps of the Garden Entrance. A film was made showing the races and entertainments. Richard started off with a welcoming speech, proposing the health of the tenants and the guests. The Lord Lieutenant, Mr Whitbread, answered for the guests and Richard, who had hidden his written speeches in a silver rose bowl the tenants had presented him with the previous evening, thanked all those employed on the estate for their support during his childhood and since his father had died in 1913. He combined this with hope that the good relationship with all would continue in the coming years. The health of the

Richard Ormonde Shuttleworth Coming of Age Celebration with guests on back steps of The House

retiring Trustees were proposed by a senior tenant who also reminded Richard that many present at the reception had been working for him for the past twenty years and more, under the Trusteeship of the Biggleswade solicitor Mr Fletcher, recently deceased, aided by both his uncle Alfred Shuttleworth and a Mr Cockburn now also both deceased, and then replaced as Trustees by his uncle Vaughan Lang and Colonel Lloyd, as well as by his mother, who, not only as a Trustee, had dedicated her life to helping run the estate. Dorothy also made a speech giving thanks for the support she had been given during all those years, especially mentioning Mr Munckton, the retired agent of 42 years duration, and the legal advisor, Mr Fletcher.

Although with Richard's coming of age, Dorothy was no longer a Trustee, she was still very involved in anything to do with the estate, with the tenants, with the villagers, with the church and of course continued to run the house. Dorothy was a very conscientious personality, brought up to carry responsibility and to be philanthropic; she imbued her children with her beliefs and was an example to all who surrounded her. Richard was permitted to follow his inclinations as regarding his enthusiasm, fascination - and ability - with all things mechanic, despite her having brought him up in a very traditional way by having sent him to school at Eton, albeit of a short duration.

Dorothy Clotilda Shuttleworth in dark print dress (Molyneux) c.1935

Dorothy was always very elegantly dressed. In the early years of her marriage to Frank, she had been taken to Paris to buy clothes at Worth or at Molyneux and I even remember in the mid-1950s being taken by her to a fashion show at one of the Paris couturiers, I think it was Nina Ricci. It was very exciting for me as a teenager to witness. We were placed on little gilt chairs to watch the models as they passed by showing off the clothes and a small card with a pencil was handed out to write down one's preferences and presumably requests to order any of the gowns.

Both before and after the second World War, Dorothy would certainly mainly shop in London where she used some of the large stores, her favourites being Marshall and Snelgrove in Oxford Street or the White House in Bond Street, from whom she would order clothes on approval to try on at home and would apparently ask Miss Willett, her companion/secretary to model the clothes so she could better judge their effect. As a small child, even I was dressed from there. I remember aged five having a purple Harris Tweed coat with a velvet collar, a matching velvet beret and the same coloured leggings which had to be knitted to match.

Molyneux was a very elegant fashion house which had also opened a shop in London between the wars and I believe Dorothy would order clothes there for any larger function. I can still remember some of her lovely printed silk dresses from the thirties, usually of a dark colour but with sprigs of flowers or small buds, which she still wore after the war when clothes were rationed. Later she would buy dresses with matching jackets in pale blues and mauves for the summer and tweed coats and skirts for the winter months. She never went out without wearing a hat, which she would decorate herself: straw in the summer with a coloured ribbon or flowers around it to match the dress she was wearing, and felt hats in the winter season. I do not remember seeing her wearing a fur coat but I presume she had one. I own a large miniature portrait of her painted in about 1910, wearing a grey fox fur, (on the cover of this book) which suited her beautifully and she had a large fur muff and matching hat made of sable, dating from before the first World War. She always wore her rows of pearls, rings and usually a brooch with every outfit, pieces of jewellery she had originally been given by Frank, and she always wore a gold link bracelet which included the keys to the safe. Etiquette of the time demanded that shoes and handbag were to match and possibly even the gloves should be of the same colour.

Dorothy was a traditional person and was very interested in history, preferentially reading books on historical subjects. She bought many books and was also a member of a lending library in Bedford to where she would usually drive once a week to exchange the books. She also enjoyed travelling – or 'motoring' as it was called in earlier times and had many guide books for the countries or towns she was visiting, which she would take with her, together with the Michelin restaurant guide known in the family as the 'greedy book'. Dorothy spoke a certain amount of French. She could converse with anyone or ask the way and go shopping.

Friends and neighbours

Mount Pleasant House, part of the Old Warden estate, lies close to the farm of the same name and was let or perhaps lent at various times to friends of the family. It is of the mid-Victorian period, of medium size and has a pleasant garden with magnificent views over the countryside towards Ickwell. The drive leading up from below the church is lined with chestnut trees. During Frank's lifetime, the house was lived in briefly by friends, William and Lady Alice Egerton. He was a racehorse owner and related to the Ellesmeres and Devonshires, she was a daughter of the Duke of Leeds and her sister was married to another neighbour, all of whom came to the Old Warden shoots or were visitors on the yachts, signing the corresponding guest books. Then, after the first World War, Admiral Sir Lionel Halsey came to live there with his wife and two daughters. They became some of Dorothy's closest friends and were very supportive to her in all things local and in the upbringing of her son. The illustrious career of Admiral Halsey in the navy included commanding a ship at the Battles of Heligoland and at the Dogger Bank. He was appointed Chief of Staff to the then Prince of Wales and accompanied him on his world tour in 1919 and then became his comptroller and treasurer and was rewarded by receiving the KCVO. After the abdication, he was appointed Keeper of the Jewel House by George VI and, during the Second World War, he was County Director of the Red Cross.

The legal firm of Halsey Lightly and Hemsley was run by the Admiral's brother and, in due course, became the family lawyers which they remained until after Dorothy's death when the firm left London, moving to Guildford. One partner, Mr Gutch Swift, helped Dorothy set up all the trusts she created during the Second World War. Of the two daughters, the younger, Ruth, was a childhood friend of my mother, Anne, spending much time together when they would be involved in various adventures and teenage pranks. Ruth was one of the bridesmaids to Anne in 1938 and led the girl guides all her mature life. Lady Halsey together with Eve Diggle were the closest friends my grandmother Dorothy had and they were in daily contact and involved in all the village activities centred around the church, the school and the village itself.

The neighbours with whose estate the Old Warden estate marches and where exchanges of land took place during the Ongley period, are the Whitbreads who live at Southill. This is an impressive house built first by the Torringtons, the landscape laid out at great expense in 1777 by Capability Brown, which probably accounts for the financial difficulties forcing the sale in 1795 when the estate was sold to the Whitbreads. It was remodelled by Henry Holland into a grand regency house. Holland had worked as an apprentice and designer in the mid eighteenth century for Lancelot (Capability) Brown. The rebuilding of the house took four years and it was decorated and furnished in the Regency style. After the Whitbreads had procured the enclosures of both Southill and Old Warden it enabled both them and the Ongleys to exchange some land and have roads re-laid, since when every generation has remained in close contact with each other. The present Sir Samuel Whitbread was a chairman of the Richard Ormonde Shuttleworth Remembrance Trust for many years.

On the drive leading from Southill House to Old Warden village is the house called Gastlings where Michael Bowes-Lyon and his family lived during the war. He was a brother of Queen Elizabeth, later the Queen Mother, who visited her relations on various occasions and I remember standing in the village as a small child waving a little Union Jack as the Queen drove past. In those years, just after the second World War, the Whitbread daughter, the youngest Bowes- Lyon son, Albi, and I were still under school age and it was organised that we should meet regularly either at Southill, at Gastlings or at Old Warden; it was quite a long walk through the park, along the village street and through the Southill park before one reached the house and so I was usually still pushed in a 'Victoria' pram.

In the wider vicinity, there were also other neighbours whom my grandmother would meet on numerous occasions, such as the Osbornes at Chicksands, the Pyms near Sandy and many others who lived in the surrounding counties.

Chapter 12

Richard the young squire, his aeroplanes and racing cars

In 1933, Richard, aged 24, stood for election to the Bedfordshire County Council and became the youngest member. His inherited sense of responsibility and his attachment to Old Warden and to the rest of the county predestined him to be involved in all local developments. Richard had received his commission to the 16th/5th Lancers but he left the army in 1930, hoping to join the Royal Air Force but was apparently advised that he was already too old. He continued flying all the same. He had bought a small plane, a Moth - whilst still serving at Tidworth, having learnt to fly nearby and had built a small aerodrome at Old Warden where he kept his planes, having already bought a Comper Swift and three Desoutters. There were many adventures and quite a few hazardous moments, some of which Dorothy witnessed and she even flew with him regularly although she always claimed she did not like it.

Dorothy had learnt to drive at an early date and, although a chauffeur was always employed, she drove herself about locally. When her son started to collect veteran and very early automobiles which he restored himself, he also encouraged her to drive in the London to Brighton Old Crocks Race, which he entered annually from 1928 until 1938 and, in 1930 she drove a 1900 Wolseley which had originally been constructed for use in India and, in the following years, she continued to enter the race, sometimes accompanied by Miss Willett. Richard had entered five cars in 1930 and took his sister Anne and Anne Adams with him: an 1897 Panhard-Levassor, a 1900 Baby Peugeot, a 1903 de Dietrich, an 1896 Daimler and the 1900 Wolsey which Dorothy drove.

DH60X Hermes Moth c.1928

Dorothy Clotilda Shuttleworth with Miss Willett c.1930 in the Wolseley - London to Brighton

Old Warden Park from the air c.1935

Richard had started collecting veteran cars which he found in hedgerows, on dump heaps, abandoned in sheds and garages, or which he was able to buy from scrap merchants. He repaired them all himself and, in 1937 drove a 1900 Locomobile steam car to Brighton, 'singing like a kettle', as reported by the press before starting the race and came first. These vehicles became the nucleus of the Shuttleworth Collection as it is known today. Richard restored them mainly himself with assistance from various friends and from an engineer, Leonard Jackson, whom he had employed in due course when he founded the Warden Aviation Company.

Soon he progressed to collecting ancient aeroplanes and one of the first he took over was a 1909 Bleriot which, together with a Deperdussin was offered to him in 1933 by a Mr Grimmer from Ampthill who had restored them to 'hopping' condition himself, when he found them with a scrap merchant in 1912 and, after the First World War, the two planes had survived in a shed on a field near Mr Grimmer's house where they remained until he met Richard twenty years later and offered them to him - on the condition he restored them.

I was always brought up on the story of how Dorothy and her daughter, Anne - my mother, sewed the wings of the Bleriot on the billiard room table, enabling

1909 Bleriot XI given to Richard Ormonde Shuttleworth by Mr Grimmer, Ampthill

Richard Ormonde Shuttleworth arriving after three day journey to collect a steamroller

that model, which was a twin of the first plane to fly across the English Channel, to be airworthy again. Richard had also discovered a 1914/15 Sopwith Pup abandoned in a field and, in order to acquire it, he had to buy and remove a whole hay rick in which the small wrecked plane was lodged. This he happily did, towing it to Old Warden and then selling the hay. The Hanriot biplane, also one of the earliest planes he found, was bought in France and taken home to be restored.

When Richard built his aerodrome, he needed to flatten the ground of the runway so he bought a steam engine at Lincoln and drove it back to Old Warden, taking three days. He was then forced to take an exam to have a license to drive a heavy goods vehicle.

The 1930s, despite the many innovations which were evolving, were at the same time full of major world-wide political upheavals: Hitler had become Chancellor of Germany in 1933, the Nazis brought in the Nuremberg laws in 1935 and the Olympic games of 1936 were held in Berlin to demonstrate to the world the success and power of the Hitler regime. Gandhi had started his peace march, whilst in 1934, Mao Tse Tung set off on his Long March, then in 1936 the Spanish Civil War broke out. In the same year Edward VIII abdicated to be able to marry the twice-divorced American, Wallis Simpson.

In 1937, the Hindenburg airship built by Zeppelin in Germany went up in flames at Lakehurst in America. This was the last of the airships which had been constructed in different countries and in which high hopes had been placed for air travel. At Cardington, between Bedford and Old Warden, the huge hangars still standing today had been built to house the airships R100 and R101. The latter had crashed on the way to India on its maiden flight killing all the passengers and so the R100 was dismantled and Cardington was used to store barrage balloons which were then used during the war to deter low flying enemy aircraft.

It was during these years that Richard was becoming involved in his various business ventures, using his mechanical knowledge and interests as well as involving himself in county projects. As mentioned earlier, he had become a member of the Bedfordshire County Council aged 24 and was considered by his colleagues to be an 'awful upstart tearaway'.

Richard had tried to negotiate building a Municipal Airport for Bedford in a field nearby on land belonging to his Goldington estate. He had flown the mayor and other dignitaries during the Jubilee celebrations of 1935 in co-operation with the Northamptonshire Aero Club from a field at Barkers Lane which lies just on the outskirts of Bedford, but it was considered to be too close to Cardington and thereby being within a three-mile danger area from where the airships landed and later barrage balloons flew.

In January of 1935, Richard opened the Warden Aviation Company based at Old Warden Aerodrome and using Heston as the Terminal Aerodrome with Archie Edmunds as his partner and Leonard Jackson as chief engineer and a fleet of three Desoutters, three Comper Swifts and three Moths. These were to be used for charter flights and he planned to offer neon sign flying and other forms of sky writing as airborne advertising to promote companies. For the latter, he formed a subsidiary company: Aeronautical Advertising Limited.

Another project he involved himself in was building Railton Cars using Hudson engines from America and he purchased a third share in Captain Noel Macklin's Fairmile Engineering Company of which he became chairman in 1939. The company produced tourers, saloons and drop-heads as well as one fixed-head coupé. The saloons were very elegant limousines, one of which was painted bright blue – 'Richard's blue' and belonged to Dorothy, presumably the model called 'Railton Straight Eight University Saloon' in which, after the war in the summer of 1946, Dorothy set off on her first post war motoring trip.

In America, where the Hudson engines were produced, the yearly changes proved unsuitable for use in England to take a sports body so, in 1937 Macklin asked Richard to help finance buying a 'job-lot' of Hudson's previous year's model at a low price to adapt for use for the English market. In one letter he writes to Macklin, he refers to the fact that he thought it quite unnecessary to have speed limits on open roads or even in villages. Probably there were still so few cars in those times and they were such a new advent to daily life that limiting their prowess seemed incomprehensible to Richard.

He had been fined on various occasions for dangerous or speedy driving and impatient behaviour when stuck in traffic. As reported in the Luton press, even Dorothy had been involved in an accident in her car in early 1913 shortly before Frank Shuttleworth died and then later, she had the crash with the Morris in France.

Richard's interests in running the estate developed in those years. He was very keen on using modern machinery on the farms and he was the first to buy a combine harvester. Richard first thought of buying an American model which would have been the right size for his fields and would have cost one hundred and seventy-five pounds but decided to support the firm his family had founded in the previous century, despite the machine costing seven hundred pounds. Therefore, in June 1939, he bought the model made by the successors to Clayton and Shuttleworth but he asked for many adaptations and, after the machine was in use, went on supplying the constructors with further suggestions for improvement. The designer came with a mechanic to Old Warden for a week to carry through the suggested alterations or improvements and, although a field could successfully be harvested in about four and a half hours, all the gates to the fields had to widened to let the monstrously huge machine pass through. This took longer than the harvest itself, but Richard stayed in touch with the firm suggesting further improvements to be made before the harvest of the following year.

Being very interested in the life of the villagers, Richard had some projects he was able to organise during the Depression and afterwards to help the work force earn by participating in estate work, such as taking the ivy off the village church, repairing the roof and adding new copper gutters.

He converted the Clock House into a village shop which sadly had to close only a few years ago and, thinking he could help employ many more local labourers in the aftermath of those financially difficult years, he tried to turn one of the ponds near the shrubbery into a large swimming pool but was forced to abandon the project as the sides kept slipping, because the earth was sand and swamp-like.

He himself often joined in work like welding and repairing the gates and started to concrete some of the driveways, as well as personally building a required cart for an old villager and helping to mend the milkman's van. He could also be very impatient though and, for instance, on one occasion he did not have the patience to wait in a narrow street whilst a lorry was being unloaded and he just pushed the lorry aside with his own vehicle. As a prank. he once pushed a slower car up a hill on a main road as my father, who was driving with him, told me.

Flying

In 1933 (the year after Amelia Earhart's much publicised solo flight to Australia), Richard flew solo in a Comper Swift to India to take part in the Viceroy's Cup contest in Delhi. He and a friend, RAF Flight Lieutenant George Stead, also flying a Comper, flew in partnership, their progress being reported by the daily papers. Having flown over the Alps, they were forced to land in the desert

Comper Swift Richard Ormonde Shuttleworth with George Stead, Viceroy's Cup

due to lack of fuel and I am told they were rescued by men on elephants, but would it not have been more likely to have been men on camels in the desert? The two pilots arrived in India, in time for them to take part in the air-race over a 700-mile course having flown for 60 odd hours in twelve days. Richard was forced to give up owing to engine trouble but Stead put up the fastest time of 153mph and came in fourth. Afterwards there was a round of festivities and, when attending the dance in Government House, Richard saw a newspaper report giving the date of a motor race in which he wanted to partake so he left the dance there and then, grabbed his clothes in a canvas bag, flew to Karachi and was able to catch a plane to London arriving in time as he had planned.

Stead flew back in due course, having completed fifteen thousand miles in all and landed at Old Warden whilst Richard's plane had to be shipped back to the makers.

Motor Races in which ROS partook

Richard's motor racing career is a subject of its own but, as his mother attended nearly all the races sitting in the pits equipped with his favourite drink of lemon-barley water, it was also an important part of her life in those years. She had become used to the fact that he would appear covered in grease from his workshop or having survived one of his numerous accidents, which he luckily seems to have come through without great damage. He had a group of likeminded friends all interested in mechanical objects, be they cars, aeroplanes, motorbikes or steam and fire engines whilst Richard was totally uninterested in society and, when he could, he avoided participating in the dances and parties given for the glittering young of that period. Even when his sister started attending dances, he did his best to avoid having to be present. Within the family there is no knowledge or even inkling of him ever having had a girlfriend, although as a very good looking, active and wealthy young man, he was certainly sought after.

In 1933 Richard drove his Bugatti in the Mannin Moar Isle of Man race. Although he was second fastest during the practice in a lap behind the winner, Brian Lewis, in the race itself he caused a smash up of the pits by skidding into them and demolishing at least three with a terrific noise before he came to stop and was forced to retire.

In 1933 and in 1934 Richard raced regularly at Brooklands, notably in the Canadian Trophy. Slim or narrow cars were suited to the banked race track and so Richard had an Alpha Romeo Monoposto 2.5 litres in which he won both the Mountain Championship, beating Freddie Dixon and then broke the Mountain lap record against Raymond Mays. In May 1935, Richard won the 25-mile handicap at Donington, beating Lindsay Eccles in a Bugatti but had to retire from the Mannin Moar race of that year due to a broken axle. In October of the same year, at the first British Grand Prix at Donington which was a Scratch Race under Continental Conditions with 120 laps over 306 miles, he came in first driving his Alpha Romeo in front of Bugattis driven by Lord Howe who was second, Charles Martin who was third and Lindsay Eccles. Fontes also drove an Alpha, Farina drove a Maserati and the Siamese Prince Bira had an ERA whilst Rileys were driven by Dixon, Brian Lewis, Percy Maclure and Dobbs. Richard, one of the youngest drivers at 26, had an average of 63.97 mph, although Farina had done a lap at 66.61 despite heavy rain in the earlier part of the day, which became sunny by the afternoon.

In the same year, Richard had participated in the Hill Climb at Norwood in his Bugatti and was fourth at the Dieppe Grand Prix in his Alpha. At the Nice

Richard Ormonde Shuttleworth at Brighton Speed Trials in a Bugatti 2.3 litre Type 51 - 15th September 1934

Grand Prix in which famous continental drivers like Novulari, Dreyfus and Chiron took part, his gear box broke and he had to retire with engine trouble. He participated in the 100-mile race on the beach at Southport but, in September of that year, he successfully broke the speed record at Brighton set up by Malcolm Campbell in 1932. One of Richard's racing contemporaries was the Duke of Grafton who was killed in a racing accident in the Irish Grand Prix at Limerick in 1936 at the very young age of just 22. He had been short sighted, wearing spectacles and, like most racing drivers of the era was totally unprotected, not even wearing a helmet. His car crashed into a wall and he suffered very bad burns and died in hospital that night. He had been a close friend of Dorothy's children, apparently a great admirer of Anne, and both had attended his coming of age party in 1935, as well as the Grafton Hunt ball at which Richard appeared by plane saying he had come to 'dance with the dowagers'. Richard would often fly over to Euston to visit the Graftons. Anne had just decided to leave England shortly before the Duke's fatal accident and did not attend the funeral as she had gone to stay in Münich to learn a further language. Dorothy flew to the funeral with Richard and they had to land on Newmarket Heath due to fog and rain and then get a taxi to take them the final part of the journey to Euston.

Richard's last race was to be the 1936 South African Grand Prix at East London. He had sent his car ahead by ship together with his mechanic, Neale, and flew there arriving shortly before the race. It was a stormy day with heavy rain and he did not have much time to get to know the eleven-mile circuit. He was also not happy about the condition of his car, the Alpha - the suspension was not satisfactory and, after a few laps, he came in complaining that the car was jumping all over the place. During the race, while going at full speed on a straight stretch, the wind blew the Alpha off the road. It hurtled through the air and landed on a flat boulder in the brush. Richard succeeded in turning the engine off and jumped out but suffered substantial head injuries and a bad wound to his thigh. He was then unconscious for nineteen days. His racing companions, primarily Lord Howe, sent an aeroplane to collect him but the local hospital would not let him go until after a surgeon had flown in to operate on his spine, then he was finally taken to the Johannesburg Hospital, arriving with a high temperature. Dorothy had been in Austria at Zell am See for Christmas with her daughter. When she heard of the seriousness of the accident, she immediately returned to England and sailed on 10th January in the Arundel Castle only arriving in Johannesburg at the end of the month. Even General Smuts, the South African statesman, enquired daily after his

Richard Ormonde Shuttleworth wins Grand Prix at Donington in 1935

health and South African friends Dorothy knew, Major and Mrs van der Byl, were continually concerned, giving assistance wherever they could. Before leaving South Africa by ship in April, Richard and his mother were invited to lunch at the South African House of Assembly where General Smuts – a small man – put his hands up on Richard's shoulders saying "Dear Boy, the sleepless nights you have given me." The van der Byls continued to be good friends and, after the second Word War and up until the mid-1960s, Joy would be lent Dorothy's house in London for a month every year to attend the London summer season.

Back in England, Richard was still walking with a stick but flew himself to Brooklands to prove he had not lost his nerve. However, the serious accident did affect him and his sight and hearing were impaired due to the damage he must have suffered and he limped somewhat from then on. He also became rather volatile, could lose his temper and was easily upset and irate. Having been unconscious for nearly three weeks, Richard had obviously suffered some brain damage because of the accident which then affected his emotional reactions.

A subsequent accident with one of his aeroplanes could also have been fatal. Richard had flown to Brooklands in the summer of 1938 in his Hanriot biplane but, when he took off for his return flight, one of the wheels came off as a pin holding it on had been removed and the mechanic forgot to replace it again before Richard left. Immediately a telephone call was made to Old Warden warning about the missing wheel and the dinner guests all rushed down from the House to the aerodrome taking a fire extinguisher with them and laid out 'SOS' in white overalls on the runway. Richard thought it a joke and landed nonchalantly. The plane did a somersault landing upside down but he scrambled out unhurt saying "Now who says flying is dangerous?"

Chapter 13

Anne grows up: her engagement and wedding

Anne was 15 when Richard came of age in 1932 and had been mainly taught at home. She was then sent to Heathfield girls' boarding school for about half a year but it was soon decided that a Swiss governess, Mlle Monet, would take her and a cousin, Priscilla Lambert, to be educated by a long trip through the sights of both France and Italy, spending many months in Florence and in Rome. Anne already spoke French, having learnt that as her first language with Pierette, her Swiss nurse-maid and she then learnt to speak reasonable Italian on their trip.

In a letter from Rome to her mother, Dorothy, in what must have been the autumn of 1934, she naively enthuses about having seen Mussolini and visited his arena with the huge statue and the Cappella dei Caduti and, with teenage infatuation, writes that she adores the Giovinezza song that the fascists had taken as their theme tune. She was invited to witness a march of the Knights of Malta under their grand-master, Prince Chigi Albani, from the Palazzo Venezia (the parliament) to honour the monument for the Unknown Soldier. It was pouring with rain but Anne was fascinated by their colourful uniforms.

She was then invited to go to an evening concert given for them at the Augusteo where evening dress should have been worn but which she did not have. She writes that this was not really a problem as the Italians were in court mourning because the nephew of the Italian Queen, King Alexander I of Yugoslavia, had been assassinated in Marseille a few months previously. She then describes the concert in detail and enthuses about the orchestra under Molinari.

In the spring of 1935, Anne was presented at court to King George V and Queen Mary in Buckingham Palace and was to do a London Debutante Season attending many parties and balls, as well as going to race meetings such as Ascot and of course attending Richard's successful motor racing events during the same year. Dorothy gave a dance in February of that year for Anne at the Upper Grosvenor Street house which had been let in the interim.

Richard did attend, although he had always done his best to avoid social events. At the end of the year, friends recommended that Anne should go to Münich to stay with Princess Weikersheim whose daughter, Mumi, took in paying guests teaching them German and showing them the sights and museums of Münich as well as going to concerts and the opera.

Although Hitler had come to power in Germany in 1933, Münich was still a town favoured by English tourists and many girls were sent, like Anne, to learn the language and enjoy the life of Münich with its opera and leading museum collections and palaces.

Being so close to the Alps and to Austria, meant that Mumi could take her charges skiing in the winter and that year they went to Zell am See, not far from Salzburg, where Anne very much enjoyed the skiing, writing home that there was so much snow. She was very excited to have bumped into Queen Juliana of the Netherlands, also skiing in Zell am See. Dorothy came for Christmas and then, after Richard's fearful accident in South Africa, left Anne with the Weikersheims again, sailing to South Africa to be with him. Richard wrote Anne a long letter from the hospital reporting in great detail on how the accident happened.

That following summer of 1936, not wanting to return to England, Anne moved to Vienna, again to stay as a paying guest, this time with the family of Princess Croÿ who had been recommended by the Weikersheims whom she had stayed with in Münich. Here there were five children, two sons and three daughters, all of Anne's generation.

Vienna had been through quite difficult and politically unstable years during the 1930s with the murder of the chancellor Dolfuss in 1934, and the socialist uprising but, for a visitor, the old-world charm still seemed intact. Alexander, the second son of the Croÿs, had been an ADC to Count Stahremberg who had raised the Heimwehr – an anti-Nazi home guard - to be active against the socialist uprisings and counteract

Richard Ormonde Shuttleworth skiing in Vilars

the increasing strength of the underground Nazi party. Alexander, known as Adi within the family and to his friends, spent part of his time at the family house in Vienna and part at his parents' estate near Trautenau in the north of Bohemia, after having done an agricultural apprenticeship at the estate of some friends.

Anne and Alexander became engaged at the beginning of 1937 but did not make it official as Alexander's father who had gone to Bad Ischl for a cure, was unwell and then died in July and was buried there. The engagement was then officially announced in mid-July and plans for the wedding started to be made but, during the following autumn, Anne developed pneumonia, which was a dangerous illness before antibiotics were developed and she was seriously ill.

Dorothy rented a chalet in Villars sur Ollon in Switzerland for six months to enable Anne to recuperate. In the meantime, her trousseau was being ordered. In those years, it was usual to equip a daughter with a completely new wardrobe and then bed-linen and tablecloths all embroidered with initials were ordered as well. An estimate had already been made in June of 1937 for linen chosen by Dorothy at Lady Ellis' company who had often supplied Dorothy with new furnishings and then had later done the decorations for her new London house. The final order was then only made as Anne was beginning to recover in November. The quantity ordered would be astonishing for modern eyes but it was intended that a young couple should be able to cater for a fully equipped household, including servants as well as future children. Anne was disappointed that all the clothes ordered had to be in grey or mauve as she would be in half-mourning until a full year after the death of Alexander's father.

Christmas was spent at the chalet in Villars and Richard came with Archie Edmunds. Anne tried to teach her brother to ski but he in his usual impulsive way just started off down the mountain with no fear and ended up with two sprained ankles. Richard had to buy crutches on the way back to England when he was driving his mother, Dorothy, in a Riley 9hp, with a snow storm, despite which they typically did the trip to Calais in just one day.

Anne's wedding

Alexander was the younger son of the Austrian branch of the Croÿ family which originated in the early twelfth century near Amiens in Picardy in the north of France. By tradition, they descended from a son of the Hungarian King Bela

Wedding group Feb 1938: standing left to right: Lady Betty Anson, Eveline Croÿ, Alexander Croÿ - bridegroom, Anne Campbell - bride, Anton Croÿ- best man, Anne Bowes Lyons, Susi du Boulay, Richard Shuttleworth - half brother gave bride away.
Sitting left to right: Jackie Swinerton-Dyer, Priscilla Lambert, Marierose Croÿ, Ruth Halsey

the Blind and then, for many generations, they served under the Dukes of Burgundy, acquiring numerous properties and titles during the following centuries and some ancestors were amongst the first members of the illustrious Order of the Golden Fleece.

Various members of the family then served under the Holy Roman Emperors. Maximilian I, whose wife was Margaret of Burgundy, granted the first princely title to a Croÿ, and Guillaume de Croÿ, Sire de Chievre, was appointed tutor and then became the first chancellor to the Emperor Charles V 'upon whose realm the sun never set'. Both Guillaume and his nephew, the Cardinal of Toledo, were poisoned at the Diet of Worms in 1521, but many further members of the Croÿ family continued to hold leading positions in different kingdoms as well as being high ranking church dignitaries. After the French revolution, the property of Dülmen in Westphalia was given them in retribution for properties lost during the Napoleonic period and the castle of Buchberg where Alexander's father's family lived was acquired in lower Austria.

Dorothy organised the wedding of Alexander and Anne which took place at the Brompton Oratory in London on the 17th February, 1938. As it was a 'mixed' marriage, the Croÿs being Catholics and Anne brought up in the Church of England, no music or singing was permitted and the bridal couple were not allowed past the altar rails.

Father John Talbot officiated and the church was decorated with beautiful arrangements of red and white flowers, being the colours of the Croÿ family. The eight bridesmaids also wore red and white wreaths in their hair and Anne herself was clad in white satin with seed pearl embroidery and carried a bouquet of lilies. She was given away by her half-brother, Richard, who led her to the altar. Alexander's brother, Anton, was best man and two of his sisters were amongst the bridesmaids, as were Anne's cousin Priscilla Lambert, and her close friends Anne Bowes-Lyon, Betty Anson, Susie de Boulay, Jacquie Swinnerton-Dyer and Ruth Halsey, her childhood friend from Old Warden.

As the bridal couple left the church, a white slipper was tied to the back of the car driving them to the reception which was held in Curzon Street and, as was then usual, many presents were displayed. The reception was attended by a large crowd of guests from London and many who had come over from Austria. The couple then departed for their honeymoon, going first to Paris and then on to Sicily.

The previous week, Dorothy had given a reception at Old Warden, held in the house and attended by the tenants and villagers at which tea was served. Alexander's family had come too and four presentations were made: a silver coffee pot was given by the Old Warden Staff and a silver kettle and tea set was given by the tenants of Old Warden, Broom, Cople and Ickwell and the organist gave a cut glass salad bowl from the choir and bell ringers.

The Women's Institute gave a breakfast set presented by Mrs Aubrey and the school children gave a rug which they had made themselves with an inscription saying 'as many stitches as there are good wishes'. Anne made her first speech – as she then said – thanking them all and assuring everyone that she would always remember them and value the presents for the rest of her life. The wedding was reported in many daily papers and magazines in both England and Scotland, as well as in Vienna.

The honeymoon was spent in Sicily at Taormina, a famously beautiful location high above the sea with splendid views over the coast and across to the ancient Greek amphitheatre. The bridal couple stayed at the well-known Hotel San Domenico in the old monastery buildings with wonderful views from all the rooms above terraced gardens leading down the steep hillside. The honeymoon had to be cut short as Alexander developed appendicitis and so they left for Rome where they stayed at the embassy and then hurriedly continued by train to Vienna where Alexander was operated on having by then a burst appendix with the danger of septicaemia.

The Anschluss took place whilst Alexander was in hospital in Vienna recovering from his appendix operation. Hitler had forced ultimatums upon the Austrian Chancellor, Schuschnigg and Hitler's troops then marched into Austria on the morning of 10th March 1938. Although many Austrians were against the takeover, there were jubilant crowds in the streets of Vienna waving Nazi flags and, when a referendum was held confirming Hitler's takeover, my mother told me she saw many of the crowd being given five schillings to vote in Hitler's favour. It was probably advantageous that Alexander who was very anti-Nazi, was in hospital at that moment as otherwise he would most likely have been one of those demonstrating loudly against the takeover, most of whom were promptly arrested.

After the wedding of her daughter, Dorothy returned to the rented chalet in Switzerland with Miss Willett, and Richard flew out to join her shortly afterwards.

Hudson Terraplane Estate Car, c.1936

When the Anschluss took place in March, they hurriedly returned to England. Dorothy drove the Hudson terraplane shooting-brake to Calais in one day, taking Miss Willett and her maid with her.

By April they thought the political situation had calmed and it would be alright to drive out to Vienna the car Richard had given Anne as a wedding present. Anne Adam drove that car, a Hillman Minx, whilst Dorothy drove the little 6hp Fiat Richard had bought her two years previously as a run-around. Anne and Adi were permitted to leave Austria for ten days and so in April they drove together to France to do a tour of the Chateaux on the Loire. As it was Easter time, it was very difficult to find rooms and Richard, having flown to Blois to join them, had to sleep on the billiard room table of a hotel and had then taken a taxi to Tours where they had arranged to meet.

Just a few months afterwards, the Nazis issued a decree demanding that every citizen's money must be transferred from abroad to the German Reich and Anne, my mother, should have complied, having gained Austrian nationality upon marriage but had thereby lost her British nationality by marrying a foreigner. Luckily any finances she owned were held in trust in the United Kingdom so it

Anne Elspeth von Croÿ, nee Campbell from the Sketch 1939

was deemed wise for her to leave Austria and return to England. Alexander, my father, remained in Austria to sort out the apartment they had just rented in Mödling on the outskirts of Vienna. He was then given a tip-off that the Gestapo wanted to interview him regarding tax evasion. He promptly decided within one day to also depart and followed his wife to England in June of 1938, presumably driving the Hillman Minx car Richard had given them as a wedding present and which Dorothy had driven out to Vienna that spring.

When Alexander arrived in England in the summer of 1938, he and Anne rented a house in Kent near Maidstone which they were able to furnish and then unpacked all their wedding presents. The political situation in Europe was very volatile all that year with Hitler making more demands and conferences were held trying to guarantee peace but, by the end of the year, Czechoslovakia had been fully overtaken by Hitler's Nazi party.

Richard had joined the R.A.F.V.R. straight after the Anschluss but he was told he was not yet needed and so devoted most of that and the following year to running the estate, and concentrating on acquiring necessary newly-developed agricultural machinery and equipment.

At the end of December that year, I was born with Dr Gilliat in attendance in the small neo-Georgian London house at No 59 Avenue Road which Richard had bought his mother, after letting the large house in Upper Grosvenor Street to the Yugoslav Government and which continued to be the Legation all during the war.

I was christened at Brompton Oratory the following January, my Austrian grandmother still being able to travel over to be present. Shortly afterwards, in February 1939, Richard flew out to Davos in his Desoutter taking the family friends, James and Chinny Adams, with him, whilst Dorothy, driving the Hudson van again, followed with Anne Adams and had a difficult journey with winter road conditions and not having enough chains for the tyres. They were there for a few weeks and then Dorothy and Anne Adams drove back taking a detour through the South of France planning to meet Richard in Paris.

He had flown back directly from Switzerland and, despite the very bad weather, flew over from England (in five minutes!) and was the only plane to cross the channel that day. There were more flights that spring and, in July, Richard had been invited to fly to Frankfurt taking a family friend, Eddie O'Brien, who had become one of my godfathers, with him to meet German Air Force Officers who assured them there would be no war.

Barely two months later, on the 1st September, Hitler's troops marched into Poland and, on 3rd September 1939, World War II was declared and Richard who was at the time working on the harvest was soon called up and sent to train at Upavon and to do a refresher course there.

Christening of Charlotte von Croÿ with parents Alexander and Anne January 1939

Chapter 14

Richard's death and Dorothy in World War II

When war broke out, Richard was just 31 and, having had the serious racing accident in South Africa a few years previously, was considered not fit enough and too old to be a fighter pilot and he himself had requested not to have to fly bombers because, as he said, his Austrian brother-in-law had many relations not only in Germany but in different parts of the continent and he would not have felt it right to be possibly dropping bombs on them. In the New Year, he was sent to RAF Ternhill and then on to RAF Benson.

Whilst Richard was still finishing his course, it was heard that the Air Ministry wanted him to go into crash inspection, which was greeted with a sigh of relief by his mother and sister. Richard came home to Old Warden as often as he could that spring and during the early summer of 1940 and on his last visit he had recounted that, if his group was to continue flying Fairey Battles, none of them would be there for much longer, as so many had recently crashed.

Richard still had to clock up more hours of night flying at Benson before he was due to take on the planned new assignment in crash inspection under his friend Group Captain (as he was then) Allen Wheeler. On the evening of 1st August, he had by chance met a cousin with whom he spent some pleasant hours before he took off in one of the Fairy Battle aeroplanes that were being used for training.

It seems that Richard and other pilots who were flying in the area, were called back that evening because the weather was deteriorating but he decided it was fine enough to do another flight and took off at about midnight. Shortly afterwards, there was a red flash in the night sky, as reported by a NCO on night duty. In 2014 a letter was written to the Shuttleworth Collection by a then young RAF corporal

Richard Ormonde Shuttleworth in Royal Air Force uniform on front steps 1940

Dorothy Clotilda Shuttleworth and daughter Anne Elspeth von Croÿ
at Richard Ormonde Shuttleworth funeral wearing blue

Richard Ormonde Shuttleworth funeral August 1940

that, during a six-week period in the summer of 1940, there had been 46 accident reports with that make of plane. They had Merlin engines that seemed prone to glycol leaks and could thereby easily burst into flames when flown on a reduced throttle. He described the site of the crash where he had been sent the next morning with the crash tender and explained that the plane must have been on fire before crashing into the hill and then somersaulted throwing Richard clear but he was killed instantly.

Allen Wheeler had the sad task of identifying Richard and organising his body being taken to Old Warden where the funeral took place at the village church. He was buried in a coffin made from oak growing on the estate, draped with the flag of the Union Jack and placed in the Shuttleworth vault with his father and grandfather. Richard's coffin was drawn on a farm wagon from the house up to the church. His mother, Dorothy, and sister, Anne, walked behind the wagon both dressed in bright blue – so called 'Richard's blue'- because he had hated black. This did cause some adverse comments at the time, but they felt it would have been his preference.

The funeral was attended by all the local villagers and tenants and many relations and friends who were able to be present. Numerous personal letters, over 500 in all, were received with eulogies and memories of his strong personality, not only from great friends and neighbours but also from those who had known him in his racing and flying world. The vicar, the Rev. E Wells, wrote in the parish magazine that, not only was he held in high esteem by those who knew him, but that he was 'tender hearted and always ready to go to the aid of anyone in trouble. He had a firm faith in God and took a deep interest in the work of the church. I know he was a man who believed in prayer'.

Admiral Sir Lionel Halsey wrote to Dorothy that, having known Richard since he was nine years old, he had watched him grow into someone always seeking to do one better, never content to just 'stay put' but always seeking to improve in all he did. He was a born engineer, self-taught and mastering everything he took in hand, whether it be the work of the estate, racing, aviation, old crocks or the work on the County Council, doing everything with a boyish zest. He was loved and respected by those who worked for him and with him, because he shirked nothing and had a heart of gold.

Dorothy was desolate, it was as if her life had fallen apart and everything she had worked for during the past thirty years had been in vain. Once again, she became responsible for the whole estate.

Just two months earlier, on Whit-Monday morning in May 1940, her son-in-law Alexander Croÿ had been arrested and interned as an enemy alien. Richard had written to his sister, Anne, that they should not have stayed in Kent where they had rented a house, but should have come to Old Warden. Alexander was put before a tribunal who assessed the internees as A. B. or C. (Category A, to be interned; Category B, to be exempt from internment but subject to restrictions and Category C, to be exempt from both internment and restrictions.)

As a young Austrian of 26, he was considered potentially dangerous having been in the Austrian Heimwehr or Home guard under Count Starhemberg, to whom he had been an Adjutant. The Heimwehr was a right wing but very anti-Nazi organisation which, in the eyes of the British, was considered to be a fascist movement. Apart from having to report to the police on a weekly basis during the first months of the war, Alexander was free to travel to London where he worked as PA to the Archduke Robert of Austria but, after Germany invaded the Benelux countries in May 1940, there was fear of a fifth column in England and 'Collar the lot' quoted by a returning diplomat set off the arrest of all suspected of being enemy aliens and people of German or Austrian nationality, as well as Italians, were arrested.

Churchill had just come to power but the heroic effort of saving 250,000 soldiers from the beaches at Dunkirk only heightened the atmosphere and Alexander was apprehended and taken to Maidstone Jail before being sent to Huyton Jail near Liverpool. Before he was sent to Australia, Dorothy and Anne were able to visit him. The internees had to board the HMT Dunera, a troop ship, which set sail for Australia taking twelve weeks to reach the destination which was a prison camp named Tatura in New South Wales. Shortly before another ship, the SS Arandora Star, had set sail for Canada with internees onboard whom the government had told the Canadian authorities were highly dangerous. The ship had been torpedoed by a German submarine and some of the survivors were then also put on the Dunera.

As the Dunera sailed down the Atlantic, a torpedo was fired at the ship, and my father told me that all aboard held their breath waiting for the explosion but luckily the torpedo glanced off the ship's side. The internees on board were a mixture of the so-called axis powers. Anyone of German or Austrian nationality as well as Italians, had been interned, and many were Jews having fled Germany and Austria before war had broken out. There were some orthodox Jews who had been mocked and badly treated by the ignorant navy sailors when boarding the ship. Some internees who were doctors of their own free will scrubbed the ship daily whilst the others were allowed on deck to exercise surrounded by barbed wire. They arrived in Perth after eight weeks at sea, continued to Melbourne where 800 were disembarked, then to Sydney and Hay in New South Wales before ending in the camp of Tatura 1 but were luckily moved to the neighbouring camp of Tatura 2 because real Nazis caused a lot of trouble with the new arrivals and so were separated. Alexander was there for eight months where the heat and the flies were most unpleasant and sandstorms ripped through the huts which were only constructed of metal with corrugated tin roofs. In June 1941, Alexander was released and embarked with thirty others in Sydney, this time to cross the Pacific, through the Panama Canal and up the east coast of the United States to join a convoy to cross the north Atlantic, at that time very much affected by U-Boat warfare. A few years later after being released, some of the internees who chose to stay in Australia were scientists and physicians and became Nobel prize winners. The young officer in charge of the internees aboard the Dunera was court martialled after the war for their bad treatment and for not preventing the theft of internees' possessions. My father was then awarded ten pounds for the items that had been stolen, although he had been able to recover some valuables when the baggage was dumped on the quay when the ship arrived in Australia.

Anne moved back to Old Warden after her husband was arrested and her brother's fatal accident happened whilst her husband was on board the internees' ship. For her the situation must have been dramatic too. Both she and her mother were in deep mourning for a beloved son and brother. Whilst Dorothy was seen to walk up and down, up and down on the arm of Miss Willett her secretary/companion, trying to come to terms with the situation, her daughter was left to come to terms with her own difficult situation herself.

The earliest memories of a grandchild

As a small toddler of about 18 months, my first memories are of Old Warden that year. War had been declared in September 1939 and 1940 was a dramatic year for the family. My memories are totally irrelevant but the vibes surrounding me must have been so strong so that as a small child I imbibed the atmosphere leaving quite clear but totally unlinked memories of every-day happenings at Old Warden that summer, be it being pushed in a pram, running in the garden or blackberry picking later that autumn.

Charlotte von Croÿ in her pram at Old Warden 1940

Dorothy Clotilda Shuttleworth as Red Cross Commandant of
Old Warden Park convalescent Home 1942

The Convalescent Home

By October 1940, the Head of the Bedfordshire Red Cross who was at that time Admiral Halsey, agreed to let Dorothy open a Convalescent Home in the House as in the First World War, but now with 96 beds. VAD nurses joined them and, by March of the following year, 52 of the beds were in use and by May there were 70 patients in the House. The hospital was for all members of the armed forces, although Dorothy particularly wanted to make it available for convalescent Airmen.

The downstairs' reception rooms had been cleared of their furnishings and hospital beds were installed. Dorothy was appointed as the Commandant and Miss Willett's sister was the matron. I clearly remember my grandmother, Dorothy, wearing her red uniform with a white apron and starched cap, or a dark blue coat and skirt and matching Red Cross hat when she went out and I never saw her in anything else until the war was over. She was, as always, very conscientious and led the hospital with her very resilient and benign way, also sticking to her own itinerary in running the estate as well as the hospital. Col Diggle, the agent, had been called up to the army so she had to rely on the help of James Robinson from the estate agents in Bedford, who would come over once a week.

Every morning, she would have the remaining employees come and report at nine o'clock sharp and gave them their instructions. She may have continued to do what she had done during Richard's life time but now had to contend with carrying the full responsibility for the estate with the tenanted farms and villagers as well as for the House now in use as the Hospital.

After the Battle of Britain and all the heavy bombing of Coventry, of London and other English cities, there was a much-reduced staff, as every able person - the house servants, gardeners and ground staff were nearly all called up for the war effort. The park was used as an ammunition dump with Nissen huts on either side of the park driveway which I remember well. A Red Cross flag flew over the house so I do find it surprising that the Park was allowed to be used to store ammunition.

Dorothy was allocated a certain amount of petrol to drive her little Fiat Topolino car that Richard had given her as a run-around just a few years previously so that she could drive across to Ampthill to the NAAFI to collect goods for the hospital. It was exciting for me to be allowed to accompany her as a very small child and I remember well sitting in the back of the Fiat which is now on show in the Shuttleworth Collection. The farms on the estate were allocated to supply milk to the country and were restricted in making butter or cream, as food rationing had been instituted.

Dorothy Clotilda Shuttleworth in Red Cross Uniform holding Charlotte aged 18 months

Hospital Ward in the House Dining Room

A year after Richard's death, Dorothy partitioned off the southern part of the Morning Room to make a memorial chapel for Richard. It was painted blue, furnished with a large oak cross made from a tree on the estate and a plaque put up in remembrance of Richard ending with the poignant and beautiful words "Love is eternal, Life is immortal, Death is only an Horizon and the Horizon is nothing save the limit of our sight", taken originally from the 17th century Quaker statesman and poet William Penn (1644-1718), but became well known due to the American author Raymond Rossiter Worthington (1840-1918). A door led from the chapel into the hall and Dorothy started to read morning prayers in the chapel for all who wished to attend, which she also continued to do once the College had been started. An organ was installed in the hall and she played the hymns herself and, at Christmas-time, she would hold carol singing evenings.

Recently the contents of the chapel were moved to the lady chapel in the village church of St Leonard's as, due to legal regulations, a place of worship may not be available when a house is registered for civil marriages, as the House now is, and so the memorial to Richard is now appropriately in the parish church where anyone can visit, and is welcome to pray there.

The Richard Ormond Shuttleworth Remembrance Trust

After Richards's death, Dorothy spent much time considering what would be the best solution for the Old Warden estate. For a while, her elder sister took her to prayer meetings where, due to a medium, she felt she was able to communicate with the spirit of her son.

On a more down to earth level, it was foreseeable to her that when the war was finally over, a private estate and large house of this size would most likely not be able to run or function as before. She was so conscious that the estate had been developed and much loved by three generations of Shuttleworths but now no heir existed.

She felt that it would be right and suitable to create a memorial giving it a charitable object. Anne, her daughter, from her second marriage to William Campbell, had lost her British Nationality upon her marriage to her Austrian husband in 1938 and, should Dorothy have left it to her in a will, and then died during the war, the whole estate would have been requisitioned as enemy property so this option was never even taken into consideration.

Dorothy writes in her small book on Richard's life: "Suddenly, at last, it seemed to come into my mind to make an agricultural college to train young men and help them to get jobs and show them a good way of life."

In July 1944, Dorothy organised a meeting of all the tenants and she told them that she was giving back the property and money to the memory of the family who loved the place. This was to be done in the form of a Trust for a College. She announced that the Trust would take boys leaving school and train them in the science of aviation, agriculture and forestry both in research and practical work.

The Richard Ormonde Shuttleworth Remembrance Trust was then founded, the first meeting taking place on 10th August 1944 at Old Warden Park. The lawyer, Gutch Swift, from the law firm used by the family, Halsey, Lightly and Helmsley set up the charitable Trust and the first Trustees there were Dorothy as chairman, Group Captain Wheeler, James Robinson, senior and Mr Swift.

To me as a small child, Old Warden was always home and I very much enjoyed going to stay and live there with my grandmother. During the time my father was interned in Australia, my mother and I shared a house near Slough with some friends who had a small boy only four months younger than me but we regularly kept returning to Old Warden. I have memories of having a day and night nursery off the back staircase with one of the many nannies who came and went. My mother moved again and again, sharing houses with friends during the war years and my father, Alexander, was allowed to return to England in late 1941 but he was not allowed to join the British Army for another two years but did war work in a factory near Slough.

In 1943 my mother, when six months pregnant, developed pneumonia and was very ill and had to be kept isolated so she was looked after by a trained nurse, Sister Rowe, who had also been the monthly nurse when I was born. (A monthly nurse was a woman who looked after a mother, and her baby also, for the first few weeks after birth.) I therefore was sent to spend probably nearly half a year with my grandmother at Old Warden as I turned five.

The much loved and long serving lady's maid, Lilian West, was sent to fetch me in the autumn of 1943 from Charmin's Farm near Redhill in Surrey which we were sharing with another family. The train journey to Old Warden entailed changing stations in London where I can remember seeing all the bomb damage and the underground stations used as air raid shelters.

I lived all that winter at Old Warden with my grandmother and I clearly remember the telephone ringing early on the morning of 30th December announcing the birth of my sister, Emma. When I was staying there with my grandmother, I used to sleep on a camp bed in her bedroom as I was rather scared of being alone in such a big house.

I enjoyed watching her doing her hair in the morning - a complicated matter of pinning up different locks of hair and then putting on the Red Cross uniform bonnet. This was a starched square of white cotton which was pleated into shape, pinned on a hat stand of wood in the shape of a head and then transferred to her head with further hair grips. The centre drawer of her dressing table was to me a treasure trove, a mixture of cosmetics, little pieces of jewellery that were not in the safe, various medals and boxes of hair pins and hair nets which were always getting torn. Then, in the top left drawer of the chest of drawers in her bedroom there was a collection of fans which she used to show me, the sticks or guards were made of tortoiseshell, of carved ivory, of mother of pearl, of carved ebony and the fan leaf was either painted, embroidered with sequins or made of lace. Dorothy had used them as fashion adjuncts in the social period of her life before the First World War and, to me they were the epitome of romanticism and glamour.

Dorothy was a wonderful grandmother. Despite running the hospital and all the other duties she had, she would find time to play with me, read me delightful children's books and take me with her when she went into the Warren or down to the Swiss Garden and even shopping for the hospital or to Bedford. I also have happy memories of a small black Shetland pony my grandmother, Dorothy, bought me and tried to teach me to ride. It developed the habit of bucking me off and usually into a cow-pat. The best moments that I enjoyed were being allowed to help unpack and refurnish the famous dolls house which (as previously mentioned) she and her then sixteen-year-old son, Richard who had broken his leg, had built for my mother more than twenty years before in 1925.

When I returned to my mother in Surrey in the spring of 1944, the bombing of London was so heavy and the planes flying overhead sounded so close that we had to spend many hours in the evenings in an air-raid shelter. The decision was then rapidly taken to move back again to Old Warden for that spring and part of the summer. The hospital was full of many convalescent airmen and I can still remember seeing them arriving in ambulances and being carried into the house on stretchers.

It was a beautiful spring that year and, on Easter Sunday a few Easter eggs were hidden amongst the daffodils in the orchard. My playmate was Michael, the son of the gardener, and I caused great merriment amongst arriving patients as I announced to all and sundry that Michael and I were engaged. Once he nearly drowned as he and I were playing at the summer house where he fell into the pond, bobbing up and down until, luckily, a passing convalescent airman saw him and pulled him out.

The girl who was supposed to be looking after us – we were only about five - had gone off with another convalescent airman for a walk in the grounds. I think she was sent home very soon after that. That summer I was given my first lessons, sitting in the summer house, by Nanny Green who had come to look after us sisters when Emma was born, and I learnt to read – "a cat sat on a mat".

Chapter 15

Dorothy, the Trust and her life after the Second World War

During the remainder of 1944 and the early months of 1945, the Convalescent Home at Old Warden continued to take patients, whilst Dorothy was already pursuing plans to open the College.

Anne with myself and my baby sister came and went to and from Old Warden, spending some autumn months in Devon before moving to stay with her cousin who had been her guardian, Jock Carr-Ellison in Northumberland where we stayed over the winter and the spring until plans were being made to move back to be in the vicinity of Old Warden.

On the train journey south, I and my sister, aged six and just one-year old, were travelling with our nanny when, as the train drew into Derby Station, a porter came along the platform opening the doors of the carriage compartments (that train had no corridor) yelling in "War's over, war's over."

Of course, there was overwhelming excitement and relief and I, as a six-year-old, first imagined that my grandmother would now be out of uniform and would let her hair grow long and that I would finally be given a pedal-car. Neither wish came true.

As the war finally came to an end with VE Day in 1945, plans were already underway to take the first farm pupils at Old Warden in the autumn of that year and to operate together with the College of Estate Management, the first principal being Sir Donald Makgill who, during the war was stationed at the Old Warden Aerodrome, being a member of the SOE.

The hospital had closed in the summer of 1945 and much of the stored furniture from the reception rooms was used elsewhere or sold. Some of the rooms were turned into lecture or class rooms and one room became a library and so the College was able to open with the first six students in the spring of 1946. Dorothy had been working hard to realise the possibility of running an agricultural College ever since she had founded the ROSRT in 1944. This became her lifework and she was completely immersed in putting all her energy into the important work she had started and of which she was determined to make a success.

In the meantime, Dorothy had first sold the London house in Avenue Road where I had been born and had bought and furnished for her daughter, Anne, a very attractive house with a large garden and some surrounding fields in Aspley Guise about 20 miles from Old Warden, as well as setting up a further trust to pay for the education of the grandchildren. She also sold the large town house in Upper Grosvenor Street, unfortunately at a very low price, the property market being still much deflated in those early years after the war. That house had been let since before the war and used by the Yugoslav Legation as an ex-territorial base for the King and Queen of Yugoslavia.

We moved into Aspley House in the early autumn of 1945. It was only about 20 miles west of Old Warden near Woburn and was a charming red brick Queen Anne House supposed to have been built by Christopher Wren but it also had the reputation of being haunted. Our father, Alexander, was still in Germany with the British army which he had been allowed to join the previous year. He was stationed in north Germany and then went to Austria where he was used for interrogation although that allowed him to see his close family again. He had only returned from being interned in Australia in late 1941

The next two winters after the war were exceedingly hard, very cold with snow and, despite the war having been won, there was rationing and at the same time a dearth of coal and even potatoes were scarce. In June of 1946, Anne had a baby son who was to be called Maxim. He was born in London and christened at Aspley that summer. The christening cake was the last of the tiers of my parents' wedding cake. It was baked again and somehow sugar was found to ice it and it was as good as new, if not more so having pre-war ingredients.

That autumn, Anne travelled to Vienna where her husband, Alexander, was now stationed with the occupying British Forces and, as said above, he was being used for interrogation, not a very easy exercise for him as many he had to question were possibly old school friends or acquaintances. Anne travelled there, on French military papers which she was able to acquire through some French diplomatic friends - as an English citizen, she would not have been allowed to go. She went to see her husband's family. Alexander's sisters and his brother had married during the war and her mother-in-law had moved from the estate in northern Bohemia which had been sold and was planning to also leave Vienna which was then under four power jurisdiction. One sister had been widowed and another had had to flee their home in Silesia when the Russians invaded Poland.

Anne wrote back regularly to her mother whom she had left in charge of her three small children, reporting how terrible life in Vienna was for the inhabitants, with hardly anything to eat and how haggard and thin all the relations were. She even went to Bad Ischl, not far from Salzburg where her mother-in-law was moving to. She did one of the journeys by train and reported on how long it took to cross from the American into the Russian zone at their check-point at Enns. Austria was divided into four zones: British, American, French and Russian under the four-power agreement.

Aspley House, Nr Woburn Sands 1947

Dorothy with grandson Maxim at his christening 1946
with granddaughers Charlotte and Emma

Aspley House proved to be too large and expensive to run without any help except Nanny and one cleaning lady so Anne, after much deliberation, finally decided to sell the house in 1949 after living there for barely four years. She put the furniture in store and moved to Austria where she had always wanted to live ever since becoming engaged to Alexander in 1937.

All the same, in the summer of that year, 1946, Dorothy decided to drive to Switzerland taking up on her old habit again of always travelling on the 'continent' as she did before the Second World War. So, taking with her myself aged seven and Anne Adams - a family friend mentioned several times earlier who had married at the beginning of the war and been widowed leaving her with two children. She had then moved to a village not far from Old Warden. We set off in the Railton bright blue 'University' saloon that Richard had bought his mother before the outbreak of the war. It was a beautifully finished vehicle, upholstered in blue leather with small niches of polished walnut veneer fitted with mirrors and matching blue carpets, all very impressive for a seven-year-old as I was then. The crossing of the Channel was very exciting for a child of seven, the car being hoisted aboard the ship in a huge net then staying in hotels, eating in restaurants and picnicking en route. We drove across France, the roads full of pot holes and the detritus of war all around us:- abandoned and burnt out tanks, tin hats lying in the hedgerows and burnt or bombed villages.

When we arrived in Switzerland, it was a huge contrast. We stayed in a grand hotel on the lake at Lausanne and I can remember the delicious breakfast with croissants which was served on the balcony of the room we had looking out over the lake. From there we went to visit a Hungarian Godfather of mine who had a villa on Lake Leman near Geneva. He had given a dance in Budapest for my parents shortly after their wedding and had been able to leave Hungary before the communists took over. I remember going to visit the Chateau of Chillon and seeing the surrounding mountains among which were the Dents du Midi with their jagged silhouette and I was teased that my teeth were like that. We then drove via Bern where we saw the bears in their pit and on to Interlaken, staying in comfortable hotels and on to the mountain village of Grindelwald where we went up the Jungfrau mountain in a cogwheel train and walked along a path on a ledge over a precipice into a carved-out room in the glacier with a round table and stools all carved out of ice. We were accompanied by Lil, the lady's maid who had been sent ahead by train to unpack at the hotel before we got there. Whilst in Switzerland, Dorothy bought some luxury items as they were then considered: silk stockings and yards of material for Lil to make up into clothes as everything in England was still rationed.

Dorothy Clotilda Shuttleworth Grandchildren: Charlotte, Emma and Maxim
at Aspley House 1949

From then on, Dorothy continued her trips to the continent. The next year, in June 1947, she accompanied us three children and nanny, by train across France. In Paris, we even had to change trains, arriving at the Gare du Nord and departing from the Gare du Midi. The last part of the journey was in a bus along the Italian Riviera from Genoa to Rapallo and then by taxi for the last part of the journey to reach Paraggi next to the well-known resort of Portofino. There a house had been rented for the family in a beautiful position high above the bay but could only be reached by climbing up 185 steps. My one-year-old brother and three-year-old sister had to be carried or dragged up every day after our outings to the beach. On the return journey, Dorothy drove back to England with her son-in-law in the Hillman Minx that Richard had given Anne as a wedding present in 1938 and Anne went by train with her children.

When my mother, Anne, had moved to Austria with her three children in 1949, Dorothy would spend Christmas with us there, first of all in Bad Ischl and later in Kitzbühel to where we had moved in 1951. Usually she came out in the summer too, sometimes by train, taking the so-called Arlberg Express but often being driven by the chauffeur she then employed.

Railton 4-door Saloon

Sadly, Richard's racing cars were sold after the war, and the beautiful Railton was sold too. I believe its consumption of petrol which was still rationed, was vast. Dorothy then had a series of Austins and Fiats during the 1950s. Later she would start going to take a cure in France at Bagnoles de Lorne and, in 1958 to keep her company, we drove to Bagnoles in my first car, a little Renault Dauphine that my grandmother had given me whilst I was working at the World Fair in Brussels. I and my siblings did a lot of sightseeing, driving around Normandy and going to Mont St Michel as well as visiting the Chateaux on the Loire. Then, the following year, Dorothy was persuaded by her daughter to take the cure in Bad Gastein in Austria not far from where we lived which was far more pleasant, particularly for us, her grandchildren, who would often stay there with her to keep her company.

The sale of the large Upper Grosvenor Street house with its mews had taken place soon after the end of the war, all in preparation for the opening of the college. Shortly afterwards though, Dorothy found that she did need a house in London and bought another house further up in Avenue Road, as she claimed that being near to Swiss Cottage and north of Regents Park made the journey from Old Warden a shorter one than if she had bought in the centre of London. The house was mock-

Tudor with a large garden and had a flat for a housekeeper couple above a garage attached to the building. It had a few reception rooms and about six bedrooms with a nursery floor above, and Lady Ellis, a friend of Dorothy's who had an interior decorating company and who had already worked on behalf of Dorothy, did it up for her in tones of blue and beige. It had harled walls on the interior, which as a child I very much disliked as jumping or running down the stairs, one always grated one's hand against the walls! Dorothy continued to spend two days every week in London attending various meetings, some about the college, as well as seeing friends or visiting doctors, or shopping or going to the theatre or the ballet of which she was especially fond and I had the pleasure of often going with her to performances at Covent Garden. She would give children's parties for us in the years after the war before we moved to Austria and, as entertainment there would be a conjuror. One year the performer asked one of the children to hand over a pound note which a small boy did. It was set alight with a match to the horror of the child but was, of course, produced whole again after a few moments of anguish.

Every summer for some years Dorothy would lend the house to Joy van der Byl from South Africa who had been so helpful when Richard had had his accident whilst taking part in the motor race at East London in 1936. Joy, who had been born in England, was a very elegant lady with many contacts in London society and enjoyed spending some weeks there after the war. Both she and my grandmother were friends of Lady Cynthia Colville who was a lady-in-waiting to Queen Mary the Queen Mother at that time. An invitation to come to tea at Dorothy's house was sent to the Queen and duly accepted. It was well known that Queen Mary was a keen collector of all things beautiful, so my grandmother prepared a small Chinese snuff bottle to present her with, which she at first graciously refused but upon departure turned to her lady-in-waiting saying "Cynthia, where is my snuff bottle?"

Some years after the end of the war, Dorothy's brother Frank moved to live in Old Warden together with his wife. They lived in Parsonage Piece, a cottage opposite the gates to the park, where for some years the Post Office had also been installed. In 1951, three of Dorothy's brothers Eustace, Harold and Frank, all died in the same year and Dorothy had a tablet put up in the village church in their memory, as she did too when her youngest brother, Arthur, died in 1957. Her sister, known to her as Dina but christened Edith, lived to well over 80. She had a small house in London off Kensington High Street and we children referred to her as 'the Great Aunt.' She had a crippled leg and always had a slight limp but, as a child, I used to enjoy visiting her and seeing all the mementos she had arranged in little show cases in her sitting

Dorothy Clotilda Shuttleworth official photo c.1950

room. She and Dorothy would meet most weeks when Dorothy was on her weekly visits to London and for some years they would attend prayer meetings together. On her 80th birthday, all her great nephews and nieces were invited to tea, and, in my memory it was the first and only time that I met all the Lang cousins together.

In 1953, the Coronation of Queen Elizabeth was to take place in June. Dorothy invited her daughter, Anne, and the three grandchildren to come over to England to witness the historic occasion. We came over by aeroplane, landing at Northolt, the first air flight for us. Dorothy had rented a window above Hyde Park Corner to watch the royal procession after the crowning ceremony in Westminster Abbey. The procession through the centre of London was both long and grandiosely impressive with carriage after carriage, as well as the coaches with the Queen and members of the Royal Family. They drove from Westminster Abbey on a long route around the centre of London back to Buckingham Palace.

The weather was appalling and it poured with rain but Queen Salote of Tonga was the success of the day, driving in an open carriage with her son, both of them of considerable weight waving happily to the crowds in the pouring rain. For the first time, television covered the whole ceremony from the church service in Westminster Abbey to the procession through the streets of London but it was only in black and white in that era. A TV was installed in the rented room so we were also able to watch the ceremony in the Abbey as well as the procession. It was rather to the chagrin of my brother, who would have preferred a different way of spending his seventh birthday, but it was an historical occasion and I am still grateful that Dorothy enabled us to witness it.

When we three grandchildren were at boarding schools in England, Dorothy was our closest relation there and, during those years, we spent many weekends with her or she came to see us or fetch us out on a free day. She was a truly wonderful grandmother, full of interesting stories and her strong, very upright personality was an extremely important influence. She was far more tolerant with her grandchildren than she must have been with her own son and daughter and to me she was a great figure to look up to and emulate where possible and an example of how to understand responsibility. Dorothy had great faith and it was her upbringing in a family with strong beliefs and the strength of duty that helped her to live the life she did.

When I was 18, my grandmother, Dorothy, very kindly gave a dance for me at the Avenue Road house with a marquee in the garden and I, and an Austrian girlfriend, decorated the dining-room to turn it into a nightclub in which a then very popular entertainer played the piano.

By the late 1950s it was seen that the house in Avenue Road was too large, the expenses to run it were very high and, finding servants to manage the house and garden had become difficult, so the house was sold in 1960 and then Anne, my mother, found a very charming flat with a large drawing room in Eaton Place in Belgravia as an alternative and a wonderful housekeeper called Mrs Bull came to look after the flat, her previous employer having just died. I was very happy to be able to live there with my grandmother as at that time I was working in London for an antique dealer.

Even in her eighties, beside the full-time work of promoting the College and the development of the Trust, Dorothy was still pursuing her old daily habits of going down to the Swiss Garden as long as she could bicycle or walk where she would still feed the ducks, and also pruned some of the flowering azaleas and roses and other plants, there no longer being a team of gardeners as before the war.

She always had dogs to accompany her, she took over Tippy, a white Sealyham terrier, which had belonged to Richard and is seen in the photograph of him taken wearing RAF uniform standing on the steps of the front door just weeks before he was killed. Tippy was liable to snap and was particularly disliked by Dorothy's grandson who, as a toddler, made the mistake of crawling into his basket.

Richard Ormonde Shuttleworth in uniform holding his pet dog Tippy, July 1940

At the same time, she had two Pekineses as did Miss Willet and then later had two honey coloured pugs who she named William and Mary because the breed, originating in China, had first come to England brought by William and Mary when they came to the throne of England in the bloodless revolution of 1688. Mary survived longest and was reputed to be able to report if a meal was ready by being sent down the corridor to the dining room and, if she came back with her curled tail up and snuffling happily, it was time to go to the dining room but, if she came back with the tail uncurled, the meal was not yet served. It is said that, after her death she continued to announce meals as a ghost. I am sure I heard her snuffling along the passage. The last dog was another pug, Sammy. He was large and lazy and, if taken for a walk would stand wheezing unable to walk any further – and he was very heavy to carry!

Dorothy Clotilda Shuttleworth in Porch at Old Warden Park with pug William and bicycle

Every year Dorothy would collect the roses when in full bloom, both from the Swiss Garden and from the Summer House, as well as from the climbers growing up the house and dry them in the airing cupboards before putting them in large pottery jars to make potpourri.

In the east wing, she had installed a so called still-room, next to the ironing and sewing room using by her lady's maid and easily available from the north corridor across the back stairs. Dorothy became interested in cosmetics before the Second World War and, realising that so many of the fashionable cosmetic companies' products were not all they claimed to be, she had their contents analysed and then started making pure face creams and lotions herself, using only natural ingredients, the recipes for which we still have, written in her very good and clear hand writing. The products were given as gifts to many friends and offered at charity bazaars and fetes being given the name of 'Rosanne' - a combination of Richard's initials of R.O.S and her daughter, Anne's name.

Dorothy continued to make her products well up into her old age – after an enforced pause during the years of the Second World War when it became difficult to acquire the necessary ingredients.

Dorothy was always busy with her hands. Apart from making potpourri and the face creams, she did a great deal of embroidery. She and Miss Willet would sit in the boudoir- her private sitting room - right and left of the fireplace listening to the BBC news every evening and doing petit-point work. At a certain time, she did a lot of quilting too.

When Richard had been born and then Anne eight years later, Dorothy made many of the babies' clothes herself. In those days babies were dressed in long flowing robes until three months old when they were 'shortened'. These dresses were made of fine muslin with lace insets and open work for ribbons to be threaded through, the clothes she had made were kept and used even when Anne's children were born.

I remember sitting threading blue ribbon through garments when my brother was born in 1946. Practical 'baby-grow' garments and particularly throw away nappies, were only available during the second half of the last century. In the years when Dorothy had her children, the baby would be bathed, dressed and fed lying on the lap of the mother – or any nurse - who sat on a low nursing chair with a small wicker-work chest filled with baby powders, creams and garments on one side and a slop-pail on the other. Dorothy, who was really very gifted with her hands, also even started embroidering with pearls and beads in her later years and made vestments and other items for the church, working with the finest, thinnest needles that existed. She taught me too and encouraged me to do handwork as well which I also enjoyed doing for many years.

In 1964, Dorothy's second grand-daughter, Emma, was married to Ferdinand Waldburg from an old southern German aristocratic family. The wedding took place in Kitzbühel where Anne had been living for twelve years by then.

Dorothy drove out with her chauffeur in her white Austin which was then used to take the bride to the church. She was given away by Alexander, her father, who also came out from England and there was an evening party as well as a reception after the actual wedding service, which took place in the charming small baroque church in the nearby village of Aurach where I have now made my home.

Dorothy at Emma's wedding with Max Waldburg brother of the bride, Aurach Church 1964

Dorothy's granddaughter Emma & Ferdinand Waldburg at their wedding, Aurach Church 1964

Dorothy's granddaughter Charlotte's wedding to Kraft Hohenlohe at Schloss Zwingenberg

The following year I, the elder granddaughter. married Kraft Hohenlohe-Langenburg and again Dorothy drove out to be present as this wedding took place in the family castle of Langenburg in southern Germany. The castle had been badly damaged by fire a few years previously but was gradually being restored - a job which took many years to accomplish, before the family could once again live in the castle. Dorothy came with Miss Willett and was able to be present at the ball given in the castle hall with Prince Philip, the Duke of Edinburgh in attendance, being the brother of the bridegroom's mother.

Dorothy still continued to travel annually to Austria to visit her daughter and she even spent some time there in the summer of 1968 shortly before she fell ill and died that autumn at the age of 89.

Dorothy must have learnt French when she was quite young. As mentioned in Chapter 11, she spoke it adequately and was well able to converse with anyone and able to go shopping when she travelled to France or to Switzerland or elsewhere on the continent. Her German was more limited but, as she regularly came to see her daughter and grandchildren after they moved to Austria in 1949, she was also quite able to understand and communicate with anyone.

Anne Elspeth von Croÿ, nee Campbell by Horst for US Vogue Nr 15689 c.1955

Chapter 16

Dorothy's later years: The College and The Collection

When the Richard Ormond Shuttleworth Remembrance Trust was created towards the end of the war, it was to include the whole estate of Old Warden which comprised at that time nearly seven thousand acres. In the early years after the founding of the Trust, some land had to be sold to finance the start-up of the College and later to support the Aerodrome with the numerous aeroplanes that Richard had collected, as well as the collection of veteran and vintage cars. Unfortunately, his racing cars were sold straight after the war.

Old Warden Park with the House and the surrounding parkland was the centre of the Estate in which also lay the Home Farm. The Village with its numerous cottages also belongs to the estate as do many of the surrounding farms: Mount Pleasant Farm is run by the college as an equine centre, Kings Hill Farm further down the back drive will now form the centre of the agricultural college farming activities. All further land, the smallholdings and the outlying farms are let to farming tenants, some of whom have been farming their land for more than two or three generations. Nearby is Manor Farm in Broom, and close by are various smallholdings farmed by Broom villagers. Between the Shefford Road and the end of the back drive is Hill House, the land surrounding it having been quarried for gravel over a period of nearly twenty years. These reclaimed fields and the new ponds or lakes will be mainly used for recreation for the nearby town of Biggleswade. The farms to the west between Old Warden and Cardington are near the villages of Cople and Northill as well as at Willington.

As from the inauguration of the Trust in 1944, Dorothy chaired all the Trustee meetings which took place once and, in due course, regularly twice a year. Miss Willett became the secretary to the Trust and always wrote the minutes. In the first

Dorothy Clotilda Shuttleworth with Nigerian Chiefs c.1954

years, the meetings took place at Old Warden and then later they were held in Dorothy's London abode. In January 1951 two new Trustees were appointed: Colonel Worsley and Alan Lennox Boyd who had been the conservative Member of Parliament for mid-Beds for many years (1931-1960) and had held different ministerial post in the Governments under Churchill and Eden – in 1960 he was created Lord Boyd of Merton. The same year Edward Bennet became the estate agent, moving into the house at the Home Farm. As mentioned in Chapter 15, Sir Donald Makgill had become the first principal when the college opened in 1946. He had been in the SOE during the war and spent some time attached to the Old Warden Aerodrome and had then headed the College of Estate Management but he resigned after just a few years and was then succeeded by Dr Miles, who left in 1953. The early years were marked by financial difficulties and Dorothy had to make a private loan as a notable overdraft had built up. At a meeting in 1947, is was decided to sell the estate of Goldington Bury on the outskirts of Bedford but the sale only went through a few years later, followed by the further sale of one of the outlying farms in 1954. Attempts were made to find sponsorship for college grants and it was suggested to amalgamate the two colleges of Agriculture and Estate management which ran side by side which finally happened in 1957. In 1959. the college was recognised as qualified to offer courses for acquiring the NDA. (National Diploma of Agriculture). Further financial problems continued to cause worry until

Alan Lennox Boyd together with, and supported by. the politician Heathcoat-Amory approached the Ministry of Education to discuss the financial situation of the Trust with its aims. More overdrafts were needed and sales of outlying cottages and fields were again considered. Necessary repair work to the House had to be postponed due to the financial situation, whilst at the same time new buildings for the laboratory and class rooms were needed as well as a hostel for the students. The farm rents had been raised in 1956 and the rise of fees for the college was talked about at various Trust meetings. Also, there were discussions about which department should pay for upkeep, for instance of the playing fields, or of the gardens and it was pointed out by Dorothy that the airfield and the farm had to cooperate and the airfield was to cover its own expenses and not charge them to the farm. Collection open days should only take place once the hay had been harvested.

During those years, the agricultural college was gradually gaining an excellent reputation, particularly after Kenneth Russell had taken over as principal in 1957, and the Ministry agreed to grants being given for special projects but wanted reassurance that the Trust was doing all in its power to carry out the work for which it had been founded. The number of students had risen over the years from starting with just six in 1946 when the college opened, to having reached seventy by the early fifties and rising steadily throughout the sixties.

Dorothy Clotilda Shuttleworth sitting with Richard Dimbleby. Standing are Jeffrey Quill, test pilot of the Spitfire, Peter Twiss, test pilot for Fairey and flew the Fairey Delta2, along with Squadron Leader Leonard Jackson and Air Cdr Allen Wheeler.

Kenneth Russell - principal c.1957

The Home Farm and Mount Pleasant as well as further land, were kept in hand. By the time Dorothy died in 1968, over 1000 acres were farmed by the college under the farm manager, David Sharpe, and the College was managed by the new principal, John Scott, who had just been appointed a few months before, shortly after Kenneth Russell's untoward death. In October of that same year Dorothy died. She had continued to chair the Trust meetings until shortly before her death.

During all the years since the foundation of the Trust, Dorothy went on taking a very active interest in the management of the estate and of the village as well as the college and it was only after her death when Lord Boyd agreed to be Chairman that the structure of running the Trust had to be modernised, particularly with regard to the financial methods of payment, and further appointments of Trustees were made. It was under the chairmanship of Lord Boyd with his wide range of influence both within the government and in the business world, that modern management methods began to be adopted. After much consultation, the Trust deed was brought up to date and modernised to enable the responsibilities to be widened and overseen by different committees who were to meet more often and report to the Trust Board Meetings which were still usually held twice a year.

To Dorothy, the establishment and running of the college founded to educate young citizens, (at first only young men, as girls only started joining the college in the sixties) had become her life work. She took a personal interest in every student, wanting to get to know them individually and, from the early years on, she started inviting small groups of students to come to the study to meet her and tell her about their ambitions and aims. She would offer them a glass of sherry and she would tell them about the estate and the Shuttleworth family and she would stress the value of living on such an estate and tried to imbibe them with an appreciation for nature. Dorothy had become very impressed by the controversial book 'The Silent Spring' written by Rachel Carson in 1962 which warned against the overuse of chemicals in agriculture which was killing off so many of nature's wild flowers and plants and thereby also causing a decline in the wild animals dependant on them, in particular bird life. Dorothy encouraged the students to read the book and to view some new inventions and developments through critical eyes. Today, reports from Natural England show how the song bird population as well as butterflies and other insects have declined massively over the past decades. I am sure Dorothy would have still been very active now, fifty years later, in opposing the overuse of pesticides, of genetic engineering of plant life and some of the modern methods of animal husbandry with the extensive use of antibiotics and other drugs. I am sure she would have wanted to see only natural methods of farming and would have rejected the unnatural chemical feeding of cattle which evolved in the following decades and which had caused the rise of diseases such as BSE. I am sure she would not have been against research in agriculture or against soil testing and she would have appreciated development on the mechanical side such as satellite tracking or more modern machinery knowing that Richard would have encouraged all new mechanical inventions and developments and that would I feel sure, have also interested and fascinated her.

In the years after Dorothy's death, as already noted, new Trustees were appointed and I became a Trustee in 1972. The Trust came to realise that a link to the founder's family was to be advocated and Miss Willett, knowing Dorothy's preferences, encouraged the Trustees to invite me to join the Trust. I felt I owed it to my grandmother to accept to try and see that her vision of the Trust was upheld despite the need for changes developing over the years. The college continued to receive government grants to help finance the education of the applying students but pressure was put on the Trust to amalgamate with another Agricultural College and, after long negotiations, Cranfield Institute of Technology took over the running of the Shuttleworth Agricultural College in 1988. In the mid-1970s Cranfield had also taken over the National College of Agricultural Engineering at Silsoe (ironically where Dorothy had been born in 1879) which had opened in 1962 at the behest of the Minister of Education. Various courses were amalgamated and the Soil Survey was also transferred to Silsoe in 1987 and in 2005 all academic activities were incorporated into Cranfield. Unfortunately, only

Students in the Saloon in the 1950s

a few years after they had taken over the Shuttleworth College and without any prior warning, Cranfield pulled out and left the Shuttleworth College without students, without grants and without tutors. It was only thanks to the huge effort of the former vice-principal of the Shuttleworth College, Professor Michael Alder, who was at that time the principal of Writtle College in Essex who recognised the potential and was able to resurrect the College under the umbrella of Writtle. The aim was to create a venue for higher education in the field of Agricultural Teaching. Some years later Writtle had, under a new principal realigned its priorities and the search began for another college geographically closer to step into their shoes and take over the still valid lease. The negotiations with Bedford College led to their agricultural and land based courses being successfully established at Old Warden, a location close to the centre of Bedford College's activities, and Bedford took over the lease Writtle had cancelled. Now further developments of the College are being pursued, the teaching facilities have been modernised, with IT available to all students, and more facilities are being developed at the campus of Old Warden. Apart from the farming courses, many other land-based and livestock breeding courses are offered to a much wider group of students, most of whom attend daily, although some still live on campus, in the hostel buildings which were built shortly before Dorothy died.

Although from the beginning, aviation had been part of the purpose of the Trust and Dorothy had initially hoped to take in students to learn aeronautical mechanics. this had proved to be unrealistic at the time and it has only been in the last decade that a way was found to take in apprentices who are taught the intricacies of restoring and maintaining historic aeroplanes. Although in the early years of the Trust, many visitors came privately to see the Collection and cars were still entered in the London to Brighton race, it was only opened as a museum during the early sixties. The Veteran Car Club had held its first rally on a private estate at the Old Warden aerodrome in 1950 and again in 1954 with ten thousand spectators.

The flying days started under Wing Commander Allen Wheeler who had been a founder Trustee and who was very aware of the importance of the Collection which Richard had built up in his lifetime. The flying days became a huge feature with around 120,000 attending and, in the meantime, some new exhibits had been acquired, either donated or in exchange for surplus items. As the years passed, only endowed exhibits could be accepted as space was becoming a problem and new hangars had to be constructed. It was of great importance and vital to continue the restoration work on both aeroplanes and cars, done at first under Richard's mechanic, Leonard Jackson, who only finally retired in the early '70s.

The founding of the SVAS (the Shuttleworth Veteran Aeroplane Society) in 1964 contributed enormously to the work of the restoration workshops, on both the airplanes and the veteran cars. It is a registered charity and was founded by two enthusiasts, Owen Dinsdale and Dennis Evernden with a further group of like-minded people. Without the expertise and enthusiasm of the group, the work would have ground to a standstill. All volunteers must be members of the SVAS which now has a total membership of 3,800, coming from all around the world and a Volunteer Workers Group which now numbers about 200. The work these volunteers undertake consists of providing help to the Engineering Department, to the Library and archives as well as, on flying days, providing display pilots, air traffic Control, ground crew, as well as Commentators and Communications Technicians. Volunteers who apply are interviewed by the chairman and by the head of department where they will work. Most Volunteers are already equipped with specialist knowledge, have skills relevant to the needs required and have achieved high standards of excellence. In 2015, in a period of just over six months, 3,000 days of volunteer work was registered. Apart from all the work done by the Volunteers, about £100,000 raised from annual membership fees is donated to the Collection and, on occasion, the SVAS will finance an acquisition for the Collection such as the vintage buses in the year 2015. Therefore, it was well deserved that the Society was given the Queen's Award for Voluntary Service in 2014. This is equivalent to an MBE but for a group rather than an individual. The Trustees of the ROSRT recognise and are full of respect for the commitment of the SVAS to the Collection and are well aware and acknowledge that, without the involvement of the group, the Collection and particularly the Flying Days could not be held or survive as they do now.

By the beginning of the 1970s, a Trustee with aeronautical experience was appointed, giving invaluable advice and creating important contacts for the Collection, the first one being Marshal of the R.A.F. Lord Elworthy and, since then, other recognised and decorated members of the Royal Air Force have given of their time to assist the public image of the Collection.

Once it had become the College, Dorothy continued to live at Old Warden Park where she resided in the north wing of the House on the first floor, which had become her private apartments. There were students on the floor above her until after the hostels were built and she was still involved in all the college's activities. She remained closely linked and involved in other local organisations as she had always been and which kept her active. She remained Chairman of the local Conservative party and she would still often be asked to do the prize giving for village fetes or for the school, even when in her eighties. She still remained actively involved in the village, be it through the Women's Institute or helping the church, such as aiding the decoration for the Harvest Thanksgiving and attending all the services.

Dorothy wrote a guide to the church which was reprinted many times. The guide relates the history and includes a list of all the monks, priests and later the vicars who served in the church with the corresponding patrons, the Shuttleworths having only bought the advowson from the Whitbreads in the early twentieth century. She describes the many monuments and memorials in the church dating from different centuries, one of the most beautiful being a carved marble figure of Sir Samuel Ongley who died in 1726 which is signed by the celebrated sculptor Peter Scheemakers (1691-1781), The great work of restoration and embellishment had been done by the third Lord Ongley in the 1840s. He bought wood carvings reputed to be from the Netherlands and even Italy. Recently it has been proved that many panels carved with three designs and the love knot emblem of Anne of Cleves really are of the Tudor period as Dorothy had always believed. It is thought they came from one of the houses Henry VIII allowed Anne to have when he repudiated her as his fourth wife. Lord Ongley had also redone the roof and was proud of the fact that no services had to be missed during restoration work. The first Lord Ongley commissioned the Ongley Mausoleum and it was erected by his widow in the graveyard in 1787, a small classical building with a lead covered roof.

St Leonards Church, c.1910

Frank Shuttleworth had also continued the work of restoration and of embellishment to the church. He had installed a carved pulpit bought in Edinburgh, donated a new organ to celebrate Queen Victoria's jubilee and had the very old church bells partly recast and two more added. The marble carving depicting Faith, Hope and Charity was erected in memory of Caroline Jane Shuttleworth by her sister and, after the second World War, Dorothy asked the renowned architect, Professor Richardson, to design a new porch to be built in memory of Richard to replace the ornate neogothic one. He was also asked to oversee some needed restoration to the roof and portions of the outside walls. In the mid-50s, the death watch beetle was discovered in the church and further restoration was needed. Dorothy had planted flowering trees along the edge of the cemetery in remembrance of all named members of the parish killed in the two world wars.

Dorothy's health was generally very good. As she grew older, she chose to be was treated by a homeopathic physician, Dr Blackie, who also treated the Queen. When she was 75, she had to have a surgical operation but recovered very well and continued to lead her life as before. She embraced homeopathy after the war. I can well remember her trying to explain to me on what the theory was based and telling me that a snake's bite could best be cured by taking more of the snake's poison in a diluted form. Although I was always interested in what my grandmother told me, I was not yet convinced or in any case sure that I understood but since then then I have adhered to her recommendation of using Arnica against any bleeding of a cut or wound and, as the plant grows here in the mountains where I live, it was a confirmation of local folklore.

In 1963 Dorothy was awarded the OBE for her work of founding the charitable ROSR Trust, with the aim of education, which she saw fulfilled by the opening of the College. She invited me to accompany her to Buckingham Palace to receive the order. Just a few days before the event, the American President, John Kennedy, had been assassinated in Dallas and, as a mark of respect, court mourning was declared for a week, so that we were to wear black. It was of course, still an impressive ceremony and I was very proud and happy to be allowed to accompany my grandmother to Buckingham Palace to witness the Queen present her with the Order of the British Empire in recognition of what she had achieved and done for posterity. The local press reported her award in the Birthday Honours and quoted her wording when she had announced the foundation of the Trust after her son's death, stressing the wish to have the highest ideals for the college and with the intention of turning out the best in technical knowledge and in steadfastness of character. The article also corroborated her involvement in many local organisations be they philanthropic, political or charitable.

On a lighter note, at about that time, I was invited to represent my grandmother and present the prizes at the annual cricket dinner of the Old Warden Cricket Club, which I was honoured to do but, having just returned from New York where I had been working for a large and important antique company, I had flown over the Atlantic for the first time in my life and suffered a certain amount of jet lag so that I did not realise that I was wearing one black and one brown shoe until I noticed when already sitting on the dais, and tried to hide at least one of my feet. The well-known MCC cricketer, Alan Moss, was present as was Bob Gale from Old Warden who also played for the MCC. Cricket had always played a role in Old Warden and the pitch is beneath the church on a field on the other side of the road. An old sheep hut was first used as a pavilion in the thirties and was progressively enlarged over the years. Matches with nearby villages are reported from the 1840s on and officially the club was newly founded in 1920 after the First World War and continues to the present day. Although Dorothy's family had lived in her teenage years opposite the cricket pitch, her father as vicar, despite having been such a famous cricketer in his youth did not play at Old Warden, but I would presume that, after the Langs moved there in 1892, his five sons played. Dorothy herself was President of the Cricket Club for many years, taking over after the death of her son, and remained so until her death.

As Dorothy grew older, going down to the Swiss Garden became rather arduous for her and, due to the lack of gardeners, the formerly beautifully kept large eight-acre garden came to be very overgrown, and gradually nearly derelict and was sadly vandalised by local youths from nearby towns, which luckily she no longer witnessed. It was only some years after Dorothy's death when the situation was becoming dire that a committee was formed to save the Swiss Garden under the admirable initiative of Jane Whitbread from Southill to whom many thanks are due. For many years, Bedfordshire County Council took over running the garden and today, after having been granted a National Heritage Award, it has been imbued with fresh life. The buildings have been beautifully restored, the plants identified and partly replanted. There is an ongoing restoration program and the historic romantic garden has become a very a popular visitors' site, lying directly beside the Aerodrome with the Collection and so is a further attraction for the many visitors. Recently, tours of the House are being organised as well to enable visitors to see all the different aspects of the whole of Old Warden Park.

Anne, her daughter, continued to live in Austria where she had built herself a house in 1954. Her grandchildren, who had been partly educated in England, were by then all grown up. The two grand-daughters had married and Dorothy had still lived to see the birth of three great-grandchildren who were all brought to see her

Dorothy Clotilda Shuttleworth's grandson Maxim and his wife Christine c.2000

at Old Warden. She continued the tradition that trees should be planted in the grounds of the House commemorating the births of family members, as she had done for her son and daughter and then also did for the three grandchildren. On the centenary of Richard's birth in 2009, three of Dorothy's great-great-grandchildren planted an oak tree in the park at Old Warden to continue the tradition.

Dorothy died at Old Warden after a short illness on 5th October 1968 at the age of 89. Her death was not only an end of an era but a huge loss to the Trust and to all the institutions she had been active in as well as to her family and to the village. Dorothy was born before the first car was invented and driven and, the year after she died, the first man landed on the moon. Hers was surely a generation that saw and witnessed the greatest and fastest developments mankind had made so far.

Dorothy's funeral was in the parish church of St Leonard, the village church which she loved and had known since childhood. She had taken an active interest in the church and the parish all her life, even writing the guide booklet described above. She had, of course, regularly attended services there ever since her father became the vicar when she was a teenager.

Dorothy was buried in the Shuttleworth vault alongside her husband and her son. A large and ornate white marble cross with carved garlands of flowers stands above the grave surrounded by a heavy bronze chain. Next to the Shuttleworth vault is the grave of her parents, the Rev Robert Lang and his wife, Adine, as well as that of

Arthur Tayler, a younger brother of Adine's who had been a tea planter in India. The grave of Miss Willett is also close by, as are those of old respected and loved servants.

The day of the funeral, 10th October 1968, was a beautiful autumnal day. The many wreaths of colourful flowers given by the family, numerous friends, and neighbours as well as from many of the attending congregation, augmented the golden colouring of nature on that day. The incumbent parson was the Rev Frank Pickard who had been the last vicar to be appointed by Dorothy, and the funeral service was led by the Bishop of Lincoln, the Rt. Rev Kenneth Riches who also gave the Address. He was a personal friend of Dorothy's and a Trustee who later became Chairman of the Trust after the death of Lord Boyd.

During the funeral service, her favourite hymns and psalms were sung and the lesson was taken from Revelation 21: 'Then I saw a new heaven,' a text in which during the long years of her life she had found much consolation. The view from the graveyard down across the fields and the park towards the House on that day is unforgettable for me. I still like to visit the church and the graveyard when I go to Old Warden and stand there and feel Dorothy's love of the place and how she made the gift of the estate as a memorial to time immemorial.

Dorothy's great-great grandchildren plant a tree at Old Warden Park in 2009 to mark the 100 year commemoration of Richard Ormond Shuttleworth's birth.

The Author

Charlotte was born on New Year's Eve in 1938, the daughter of Alexander, Prince Croÿ and his wife, Anne Campbell, who was the daughter of Dorothy Clotilda Shuttleworth. She spent much of her childhood at Old Warden Park. In 1949 she moved with her mother and siblings to Austria but was sent to boarding school in England, always looked after by her grandmother, Dorothy. After working for some years in the art market, she married and had three children and lived at Langenburg in Germany for twenty-five years. After her divorce, she worked for the international auction house, Christies, in Germany for twenty years. Having married again in 1993, she and her husband retired to Austria in 2000, where, after being widowed, she still continues to live.

After her grandmother' death she became a Trustee of the Richard Ormonde Shuttleworth Remembrance Trust which she remained for nearly forty years and, after retiring from being a Trustee, she was appointed Patron to the Trust.